Criminal Behaviour, Prisons and Prison Reform

Police and Crimin

Initial Title:
'Can Active Engagement in Sport Reduce Criminal Behaviour'

A Literature Review - September 2001

Edited updated and submitted by
Edd King and the Author D. Cochrane.
[June 2019]

Copyright © David Cochrane 2001

Revised Title:

Criminal Behaviour, Prisons and Prison Reform in the UK

The right of David Cochrane to be identified as the Author of this work has been asserted by him in accordance with the Copyright, Design and Patents Act 1988 and any amendments thereto or re-enactments thereof in so far as they enhance or preserve the Author's rights.

All rights reserved.

No part of this publication may be reproduced stored in a retrieval system or transmitted in any form or by any means without the prior written permission of the Author or be otherwise circulated in any form of binding or cover other than that in which it is published and without a similar condition being imposed on any subsequent purchaser.

David Cochrane, MSc; MRes; Cert. Ed; Cert. Couns.
Originally submitted in 2001 as partial requirement for the award

of

Master's in Police and Criminal Justice Studies
University of Portsmouth

**Updated and submitted as a reference for students of
The Criminal Justice System. DC 2019**

The author is ex-forces and a retired lawyer. His second Master's researched HM Forces summary justice system and he now undertaking research into the Armed Forces retention of personnel. He his legal career dealing with criminal work, as will be seen from his empirical evidence [at 8 hereof]. He found that prison inmates needed education and engagement with different peer groups and environments; punishment was not the way to deal with most of them. So why were they in jail? The author is an exponent of the idea that prison does not work, and that sentences of less than twelve months are pointless. In cases involving violence, where there is a clear need to protect the public, then short sentences are obviously no deterrent. The prison service cannot carry out the aims it was established to do, viz; *'to help those sentenced to custody to lead law-abiding and useful lives ...'* as, over a short period there can be no effective rehabilitation or worthwhile education programme as there is a shortage of education staff and the education budget is too small; there is almost uncontrolled violence and drug-abuse in prison and a shortage of prison officers. All a short sentence does is remove the fear of prison as a deterrent, so is totally counter-productive. Look at the Civitas report *'Who Goes To Prison'*. Recidivism looms large and costs the UK £13b pa. [2016 figure]; seventy percent of prison sentences are imposed on criminals with at least seven previous convictions. And fifty percent are imposed on offenders with fifteen or more recorded crimes. Fewer than one in twelve prisoners are inside for a first offence, but that still amounts to around 7,000 people. and where they are in jail, it is usually for a crime of extreme violence or sex offences. That is encouraging but raises two points. One; offences of violence do not warrant a short sentence and two, who, then, would be serving short sentences? It seems that for extreme violence / sex offences, a longer term is reasonable, and it is pointless to jail a person for e.g., a serious speeding offence, or a person [see supra] unlikely to re-offend [such as Jonathan Aitkin or Lord Archer, or maybe lawyers and other professionals who rarely pose a danger to the public. Nobody should go to jail for a first offence [except where there is a danger to the public, obviously] and any sentence of up to twelve-months, and certainly six months or less, is pointless so other sanctions should be imposed where a period of probation or community service may well have a deterrent effect, and overall do more good, and be substantially cheaper, than a spell in jail. There might be a case for all sentences of six months [or even a year] or less being wiped from the offenders' record to give all those so effected a fair 'second chance'. [Read 'Nelson's Law' [Edd King]; it gives a fuller insight into first-offences, the use of prisons and 'second chances' It is a work of fiction, but the writer makes some very valid points on this subject, nonetheless. moduk2011@gmail.com

CONTENTS

Abstract

1. Introduction
    1.1 Aims
    1.2 Antisocial and Criminal Behaviour
    1.3 Sport
    1.4 Juveniles
    1.5 Diversion
2. Why Social Crime Prevention?
3. Sport as Prevention
4. The Evidence
    4.1 Outdoor Prevention Programmes
    4.2 Sport; The Opportunities
5. The Offender
    5.1 The Offending Character
    5.2 Sport and the Offender
   Crime Prevention Initiatives
    5.3 Community Developments
    5.4 The Police Role
    5.5 Rehabilitation of Offenders
    5.6 A New Initiative
6. In-depth Review of Prevention Schemes
    6.1 Solent Sports Counselling Project
        6.1.1 General
        6.1.2 Client Profile
        6.1.3 Success?
    6.2 A French Success?
        6.2.1 General
        6.2.2 Client Profile
        6.2.3 Success?
7. Empirical Input
8. Conclusion
9. Bibliography

In the main, statistical findings provide no support for the argument that sport and participation in sport are effective mechanisms of crime control. But that is as much to do with the methodological problems of research design and of controlling variables as anything else. After all, there is very little clear-cut evidence that any crime-control strategy is effective.

[Jupp. V[1]]

Abstract

[1] Jupp, Victor 1 'Sport and Society'. Criminal Justice Matters No. 23, 1996 pp 24 & 25]

It is difficult to conceive of anybody who cannot benefit in some way by engaging in competitive games and physical exercise in an environment shared with others pursuing similar pastimes and involving themselves in their interpersonal relationships and social intercourse associated with sport. Whether it will also reduce in juvenile pre-deviants their inclination to engage in antisocial and criminal behaviour is a difficult question to answer definitively, but this dissertation will consider the benefits of sport, the various schemes formulated to dissuade juveniles away from crime and antisocial behaviour and their varying degrees of success.

A strong sports-orientated lobby may offer vapid assurances that sport can reduce offending but fails to provide convincing evidence; some academics are less positive about the benefits, and other persuasions are content to allow the agencies of law and order to deal with offenders. Sport may be just one of the many mediums through which pre-deviants can be 'diverted' and that any mission promulgated with this objective and managed along accepted lines of engagement, education and supervision will possibly succeed.

All one can do is to sift through the available evidence and come to our own conclusions. There may be some element to be found exclusively within the sporting environment which is beneficial to at-risk youngsters but whether it is the degree of risk and competition found in outdoor pursuits which replaces the excitement to be found in law-breaking, or the discipline and society of others similarly occupied or possibly just exclusion from ones habitual surroundings, they all have to be considered. Faced as this country is with the rising crime rate [knife crime[2]] and the supposed increase in secure places for young offenders, the authorities must commission serious, in-depth research into the value of sport as a deterrent to crime. The cost in financial terms, the wasted lives and the unrelenting attack on the fabric of society which crime poses, must be addressed. It should prove beneficial, then encouragement to begin and continue a lifelong interest in sport will have to begin with children of primary-school age if the benefits are to be exploited to the full.

Jupp has already concluded that there is no evidence to support the hypothesis that sport can divert juveniles from crime; this dissertation serves to agree with his findings, but with the caveat that it is only because of insufficient large-scale research, and not because research so far undertaken proves that it does not. The researcher has only to undertake on objective presentation of the facts and allow the reader to come to his or her own conclusion.

Sporting activity can improve the physical and well-being of all of us; this is beyond argument and there is little to suppose that juvenile delinquents are somehow immune to such benefits; proving they are not is another matter.

1. Introduction.

---

[2] In the year ending March 2018, there were 285 knife-related murders in England and Wales. Around half of males injured by knife crimes, and half of the male perpetrators, are black and under the age of twenty-four. They also are more likely to be poor, excluded from school, and vulnerable to mental-health problems.

1.1 Aims.

Regrettably, time and financial constraints prohibit a full original research programme into this wide-ranging and multi-faceted topic but this dissertation, a literature review, will present the reader with sufficient information to enable him or her to establish, if not whether sporting activity is efficacious in diverting 'at-risk' juveniles and offenders from anti-social, offending and re-offending behaviour [hereinafter 'offending behaviour, then certainly that further research into the subject might be of value. The content of the reviewed texts is tempered with the writer's experience over many years as a lawyer [criminal inter alia] and the obvious involvement with, and counselling of, offenders some of whom were in custody, and of his lifelong engagement with diverse sporting activities.

The aims are not to be easily achieved, as there are considerable methodological difficulties for the original researcher not least of which is the inability to maintain a credible control group due to the multitude of variables over which the researcher has no sway. The value of the dissertation will depend on the readers' own purposes, but it will at least enable them to make some informed decisions or to present some worthwhile arguments and conclusions to their colleagues.

With this aim in mind, the parameters of the discussion will be defined, followed by a discussion on why society should concern itself with diversion rather than just allowing the forces of law and order to engage with and punish offenders. The concept of sport as prevention and available evidence relating thereto will be investigated and thereafter a consideration of the material – 'the clients' – that various initiatives have to deal with and the challenges they pose. Several crime-prevention schemes based on sport will be looked at followed by a more detailed survey of some successful schemes.

Throughout this paper, reference will be made to a number of terms which, unless defined, could skew the concept and aims of this dissertation so undermine the integrity of the paper and dilute its value in its aim of aiding the reader to arrive at a meaningful evaluation of the evidence.

1.2 Antisocial and Criminal Behaviour

Antisocial behaviour; '... behaviour opposed to principles or instincts on which society is based or to normal social practices; not sociable'. [COD]. Antisocial behaviour is not criminal behaviour *per se*, though certain crimes could also be antisocial; it is generally just a nuisance. Even responsible adults engage from time to time in such behaviour, some just through thoughtlessness or by accident and others through deliberate acts which may or may not constitute a tort[3]. As children, we have all engaged in such conduct at some time but fortunately most of us, by diverse means, e.g., by a spanking or being sent to our bedrooms or having a clip round the ear, learned to appreciate that such conduct is not acceptable or conducive to good neighbourliness and we desisted. It is worth considering how much of a deterrent those 'diverse' means were, and whether, had they been lacking in our upbringing, society may have experienced a deterioration in our behaviour to the extent that we engaged in – or in

---

[3] A tort is a civil wrong independent of contract and liability arises from a breach of duty primarily fixed by law towards others generally and which is redressable by a claim for unliquidated damages, i.e., compensation.

more – criminal activity.

Whether behaviour is or is not antisocial is a subjective determination and one which depends on the neighbourhood; what is a 'nuisance' in the leafy avenues of Camberley in Surrey may be of no concern to the residents of Stratford, East London. Unfortunately, it is when antisocial activities escalate in frequency and degree of damage to the fabric of our lives that they can become criminal acts. Coalter[4] [p.1] under the heading 'The Need for Conceptual Clarity' put it thus;

'What behaviour is included in the notion of 'antisocial'? Delinquent behaviour varies from petty, often opportunity-led vandalism [graffiti, damaging telephone boxes, systematic stealing [cars, housebreaking] and drug abuse[5] to crimes of violence. The absence of consensus about such definitions greatly limits our ability to compare research findings'

Here, then, we must use our good practical sense of everyday affair, and our own terms of reference to decide what we understand by it. All the examples Coalter gives are criminal acts [of varying seriousness] but not all necessarily antisocial as well. However, for the purposes of this dissertation we will frequently refer to antisocial conduct because if we are able , via sport, to reduce its incidence by encouraging youngsters to refrain from [all but the most innocuous] antisocial behaviour, then the implications are that they will not graduate to degrees of antisocial activity which, by its very nature, amounts to criminal behaviour.

Criminal behaviour; Behaviour punishable by law. This paper is principally concerned with the crimes committed by juveniles.[who

---

[4] Coalter, F., Sport and Antisocial Behaviour; a policy review. Research Digest no. 41 The Scottish Sports Council, Edinburgh [1996]
[5] See http://www.emcdda.europa.eu/countries/drug-reports/2018/united-kingdom_en

commission by far most offences; [HMSO 1991[6]] To concentrate on juveniles and their diversion and rehabilitation means that, by implication, most offending will be covered. However, only relatively few offences committed by youngsters are recorded and the statistics show that of all vandalism only 10% of offences are recorded, wounding only 21%, theft from a motor vehicle, 86% [NB insurance claims which generally follow such thefts account for this high number. [Mayhew, et al, p.15[7]]. It is easy to appreciate the enormity of the problem for the general ,public and the massive dilution of police resources that would occur if all cases were reported, let alone investigated[8].

More startling, only about 4 in 100 offenders are convicted or cautioned, [Mayhew *et al, ibid;* and Wilkinson[9]]. In simple terms, the nuisance value of crime alone, not to consider the expense to the citizens of this country and to businesses, is higher than most people realise. The Home Office frequently acknowledges that crime costs the country tens of billions of pounds annually, so the cost is greater when accounting for the 'hidden' crime.

1.3 Sport

Sport; All forms of physical activity which, through casual or organised participation aims at expressing or improving physical

---

[6] HMSO A Digest of Information on the Criminal Justice System. HMSO London [1991]

[7] Mayhew, P; Elliot, D and Dowd, The British Crime Survey HMSO [1989]

[8] Nearly 10,000 crimes, including violent crimes, sexual offences and domestic abuse, have gone unrecorded [Report by Her Majesty's Inspectorate of Constabulary and Fire and Rescue Services].

[9] Wilkinson, J; British Journal of Social Work; Using a reconviction predictor to make sense of reconviction rates in the probation service. 24[4] pp 461-475 [1994]

fitness and mental well-being, forming social relationships or obtaining results in competition at all levels. [Council of Europe, European Sports Charter, 1993]. This is a wide definition of sport that extends far beyond traditional team games, to incorporate individual sports and fitness-related activities such as aerobics and certain dance activities as well as recreational activity such as long walks and cycling [The Value of Sport – Sport England 1999]. Robins pp. 6-7[10] put it thus; *'Conceptions of what actually constitutes sport vary greatly'*. Of the schemes he surveyed he concluded *'The most popular competitive team game in the world , football, predominates'*. But there isd also participation in basketball, biking, boxing, canoeing, swimming, rock-climbing, abseiling, hiking, weight-training, physical training and fitness courses and general outdoor pursuits; these outdoor activities will be considered separately. On some schemes, which Robins looked at, 'sport' also included snooker, pinball and computerised games. *'... sport is used a generic term encompassing an extremely wide range of physical activities and recreational pursuits ...'* At the far end of the scale he found a definition of sports and games as *'... just activities people do because they enjoy them ...'* which presumably includes anything, anywhere as long as it cannot be regarded as being antisocial or criminal[11].

'What is implied by 'sport'? '... physical exercise [aerobics, climbing, swimming] partner sports [squash, badminton, tennis] or competitive team games? Each of these involves different social and psychological processes, challenges and skills and therefore will address differing aspects of the causes of 'antisocial' behaviour ...'
[Coalter, p.1]

---

[10] Robins, D; Sport as Prevention; The Role of Sport in Crime Prevention; Programmes Aimed at Young People . Centre for Criminological Research, University of Oxford [1990]
[11] We have to here judge by normal 'UK' standards; in some countries spitting in the street is 'normal' but in the UK it is antisocial behaviour; in some countries, the age of consent is younger than the UK; some religious practices in the UK are both criminal and antisocial by UK standards.

Lower working-class 'estate' youths were '... thrown back onto, and became uniquely over-reliant on, a 'narrow range' of cheap commercial activities' [Robins quoting Hargreaves[12]] and which the Sport England[13] surveys indicated were activities not normally identified as being 'healthy' but those which can be enjoyed on a casual, unorganised level but not including pastimes associated with the pub, e.g., darts, snooker or cards, or in an amusement arcade.

1.4. Juveniles

This is a generic title which includes all youth up to the age of 25 years [not strictly 'juveniles' but the age at which most offenders, except those who move into the category of persistent, career-offenders, have grown out of offending behaviour] but with no minimum age although one generally associates youngsters of 14 years and upwards ass coming within the band most likely to offend. The peak for males in 1971 was 14 years, although it has now increased to 18. [Newburn[14]]

Although it is well established that most people convicted of crime come from working-class and lower-class backgrounds, [Rutter and Giller[15]] self-report studies, which give information on 'hidden' crimes,, i.e., those which are not reported or for which no person has been apprehended, indicate that offending is far more widespread across all

---

[12] Hargreaves, J; Sport, Power and Culture. Cambridge University Press [1986]
[13] Sport England. Best value through Sport; the valuer od sport . London. [1999]
[14] Newburn, T; Youth Crime and Justice; Young People and Crime . Oxford handbook of Criminology . Maguire, M, Morgan, R and Reiner, R [Eds] OUP [1997]
[15] Rutter , M and Giller, H; Juvenile Delinquency; Trends and Perspectives , London, Penguin Books [1893] .

classes that the official statistics indicate, though these relate to relatively minor crimes and only very few admit to persistent offending [Rutter and Giller, ibid; pp. 27 – 29].

The children of professional classes are less likely to offend or to become persistent offenders and this can be appreciated in considering that they perform far better at school than the lower socio-economic groups, achieving a 70% success rate in GCSEs with good grades compared with 14% of the lower, poorer working classes. Another useful statistic is that 80% of university students are from professional, managerial classes, whilst only 17% are from the lower socio-economic group [Government report, 2001 – no further reference]. This does by no means suppose that we ought to discount the higher-performing sections of society as being beyond any potential benefits of a suitable sports-based programme, as endeavours to curtail the [albeit small] contribution they make to the antisocial element and to the petty-crime figures, will certainly make an impression on the crime statistics and, ultimately, to the law and order budget.

Most persistent offenders are likely to originate from the lower socio-economic groups, as we have already said, and are also those less likely to move early into paid work. It is noted that gainful employment is the most likely reason for offenders curtailing their offending behaviour. [Braithwaite[16]]. For a fuller discussion on the characteristics of the persistent offender see part 5 [infra].

Dr George Cary, the Archbishop of Canterbury said in September

---

[16]Braithwaite, J; Crime, Shame and Reintegration. Cambridge University Press. [1989]

1991[17], when commenting on the Tyneside riots of the summer of that year, 'Human wrongdoing is inextricably linked to social deprivation, poverty, poor housing and illiteracy ...' Notwithstanding, all youth up to the age of 25 years and from all social backgrounds should be considered as possible beneficiaries of the sports programmes within the context of this dissertation.

1.5. Diversion.

Diversion is becoming the dominant trend in many countries in their dealing with juvenile crime and apart from any other benefits it reduces the risk of 'labelling' offenders as 'criminals' – the theory that crime is not an independently existing phenomenon, but a label attached to certain forms of behaviour. Becker[18] and Gelsthorpe[19], et al, noted three forms of diversion. Viz., [a] *diversion from crime* by prevention, achieved by the use of activity groups, provision of leisure facilities and social crime prevention measures targeting the 'at risk' groups and which embrace '... *any programme that can claim to affect the behaviour pattern, values and self-discipline groups seen as having the potential to offend ...*' [Gilling[20], p.5] and [b] *diversion from court* which for offenders promotes the use of discharges, warnings, cautions and community-based interventions such as intermediate treatment [IT] effected through a series of projects established by voluntary bodies in various local authority areas serving [inter alia] as an alternative to prosecution and [c] *diversion from imprisonment* or

---

[17] Carey; G, Archbishop of Canterbury, also attacked Howard's policy on crowded jails in a Daily Telegraph article [8 April 1995]. See at 2 Why Social Crime' below,
[18] Becker, H.S., Outsiders: Studies in the Sociology of Deviance. London. [1963]
[19] Gelsthorpe, L. R. Diversion in English and Dutch Juvenile Justice in Fennell, P., Harding, C., Jorg, N., and Swart, B., [Eds] The Europeanisation of Criminal Justice. OUP[1994]
[20] Gilling, D., Crime Prevention Theory, Policy and Politics. University College London Press. [1997]

young-offenders' institutions [YOIs] which encourages the use of community-based programmes, i.e., 'heavy-end' IT and community service orders instead of incarceration [Cited Atherton[21] p.10]

2. Why Social Crime?

Many observers believe that prison does not work and that it can be destructive of any redeeming features which could otherwise be teased from deprived youth. Cary [1995] set out a very keen criticism of prison as being a reforming institution. 90,000 people are sent to prison each year, and of those released two thirds will return, many within one year of release.[22]

Alternatives to custody should be explored and more effort expended in prevention of crime. With the various mechanisms in place to deal with adult and juvenile offenders, and the associated welfare and probation services, there is already adequate provision to deal with young criminals. Unfortunately, these bodies do not engage with the youth until the commission of a crime and therefore they ndo not operate to deal with pre-offending behaviour which may be merely antisocial but is in many cases the prelude to offending activity.

That apart, we should take account of the predictors of criminal behaviour and take all reasonable precautions to divert our juveniles away from crime because we are a moral, civilised community and society has, in many cases, already failed our at-risk youngsters. The

---

[21] Atherton, J., Outdoor Pursuits Courses and Young Offenders. University of Cambridge. Unpublished dissertation for award of MPhil., Criminology. [1994]

[22] For the latest information on crime and justice in England and Wales, look at the Office for National Statistics, in particular 'Proven Reoffending' April 2018.

detaining of offenders is costly and is becoming ever more expensive[23]. Prisons are unable to offer the facilities as advertised; diversion and reform represents a better deal for all concerned; formal court proceedings and detention can have harmful effects and, lastly, the majority of juvenile offending is minor and transient. These aspects are hardly contentious as the supporting evidence is overwhelmingly in agreement.

The UK processes of law and order with its prisons, YOIs and various community provisions, do expose offenders to whatever rehabilitation and education services are established to deal with their offending and encourages them to address their behaviour. But consider the following passage :-

> 'Criminals choose to commit crime; crime resides within a person and is caused by the way he thinks, not by his or her environment. Criminals cause crime – not bad neighbourhoods, television, schools, drugs or unemployment. Crime resides within the minds of human beings and is not caused by social conditions.'
> [Tame[24]]

If these sentiments were predominant and evidenced by proper research, one could argue against any efforts to reform offenders. Likewise, anything other than punishment meets with the response, 'Why should we afford these young criminals the use of facilities and extend other benefits which the young, law-abiding kid on the street is very probably denied?' Those who cynically dismiss the ideas of

---

[23] It costs £63,000 pa per prisoner at HMP Frankland; it costs half that to keep a prisoner in Durham jail.

[24] Tame, C. R., 'Freedom, Responsibility and Justice; The Criminology of the New Right' in Stenson, k., and Cowell, D., [Eds] 'The Politics of Crime Control. London. Sage [1991]

diversion and of offender rehabilitation should be reminded of the annual law and order budget, and that in 1998 it was reported that the taxpayer was facing a £2bn bill for the construction of 24 new prisons.[25] There are presently [July 28th 2001] 66,611 men and women in our prisons, an all-time high. In 1993 it was 42,000; in 1996 it was 54,600. In the year 2000 only 3,000 inmates were involved in any rehabilitation schemes including programmes for sex offenders [600] and the remaining 2,400 places were concerned with drink-related offending, domestic violence, and anger-management.[26]

Of all prisoners discharged in 1993, 53% were reconvicted within two years, as were 89% of 15 to 16 year-old males discharged from youth custody. Of *all* male 73% were reconvicted within seven years. [HMSO[27]]. The reconviction rates are not surprising in a culture which allows half of the young offenders leaving Portland YOI [for example] to return to living on the streets[28] and then denying accommodation to ex-offenders[29]. ['and in the text adding '... burglars and other criminals are to lose their right to a local authority home in a Government attempt to rid large estates of trouble-makers' – presumably stating this as the justification. This policy has since been reversed, as it clearly would have caused more problems than it would have solved. But nevertheless, the very fact that it ever existed says a lot about how the authorities perceive the problem of crime in the community.

---

[25] Daily Telegraph, January 29th, 1998, anon]. In 1996 the figure for new prison construction was £1bn. The cost of running the prisons already commissioned [2001] rises by £1bn per month.
[26] Association of Chief Officers of Probation, January 2000. The population at May 2019 was 82,707; approximate ratio men to women is 22 to 1. [Retrieved from the HMPS website 25/05/19]
[27] HMSO Statistical Bulletin 5/97 'Reconviction of Prisoners, England and Wales. London [1997]
[28] Ramsbotham, Si David, Chief Inspector of Prisons [March 2000]
[29] 'Criminals set to be denied council homes' headline, Sunday Telegraph, 21 November 1999 [anon]

Nor can inmates rely on receiving education whilst in jail, education which would enhance their prospects of reintegration into society and getting a job, as the prisons' education budget has been cut in recent years. In 1997 the 'prison education bill' [sic] was £36.2 million [Tilt[30], and Butcher[31]]. And in 1997, Chairman, Association of Prison Education Contractors, cites a £2.6m reduction in the education budget over the previous two years.

But what do the offenders themselves say? Of the hundreds of hours, the writer [a former criminal lawyer] has spent talking with old and young inmates and former inmates, the only fear prison held for them was the apprehension they felt when taken down for their first spell in prison. They soon learned, within days that in most cases, prison was 'a doddle'; that their worst fears were unfounded and that many were getting three hot meals every day. As one young offender put it :-

'Unless they string me upside down and whip me, prison isn't a deterrent. It's what I'm used to. You sit in your pad and you get gym and football. You can do without your freedom. There's nothing for me out there. I've no choice but to come back.'
[Telegraph Magazine, January 1998]

From interviews, it transpires that life 'inside' is easy, and they also get paid. C and D category prisons have libraries, sports facilities, some have acres of grounds under cultivation, some with beautiful gardens and places of worship. Inside they engage in 'para-social' relationships [as it is doubtful they make real friends] but they find a niche for themselves and, whereas they find it advisable not to 'buck

---

[30] Tilt, R., 'Reformation lies in jail education' Telegraph, 22 December 1997
[31] Butcher, J., R., 'Jail Education' Telegraph 22 December 1997

the system' they are credited with a good deal of 'street-cred' on their release into [almost invariably] the social circles which they previously and so suddenly vacated for a term an Her majesty's pleasure. Where such a mind-set exists, it is obviously difficult to attempt any meaningful rehabilitation without some genuine long-term help with education and 'social realignment'.

Not many leave prison as reformed characters and many harbour some skewed idea that society now 'owes them' because 'it' or 'they' [the public conscience] has put them into prison. Conversely, the prospect of returning to prison holds no fear for them. The system has 'wet it's powder' if it hoped to exploit the advantage, the deterrent of apprehension the first-timer feels when committed, or might face, prison, and that advantage will never be regained. The only prospect society now has without expending effort in reform is that the offender will grow out of crime, which hope will be enhanced if society in turn is prepared to accept him back, along the lines of Braithwaite's [ibid] 'reintegrative shaming' where '… offenders are encouraged to accept that they have done wrong while society readmits them. [Cavadino and Dignan[32] p. 44].

The damage criminal activity inflicts on the fabric of society is incalculable. A child who comes from a home without a father figure such as where the father is in prison, is a child who mis more likely to finish up in trouble with the law, especially where on or other or all the conditions apply, viz., poor educational attainment, poor housing and , exposure to substance abuse. This list is not exhaustive by any

---

[32] Cavadino, M., and Dignan, J., 'The Penal System: An introduction. London, Sage [1997]

means, the temptations frequently encountered and known to even the most cursory glance into the study of criminology. To this extent, crime breeds its own culture, although recent evidence suggests that any damage caused by lack of a father-figure in early social relationships is not permanent and can be repaired by positive links with other adults. [Ainsworth and Pease[33]].

We already have the highest prison population in any EU country except for Portugal; there are 11,000 prisoners under the age of 18 years [2001 figure] and each place costs around £24,500 pa, though a 2001 estimate by the Howard League for Penal Reform put the figure at £27,000.[34] Holland, by contrast, has a very low-level of custody, and a relatively low level of crime [Currie[35]]. Prison is nothing if not costly, and some commentators believe it does not work. If a fraction of this money were to be invested in education outside prisons for deviants in the community and in social crime prevention a great deal more might be achieved.

It is time to consider effective methods to prevent offending in the first place and thereby reduce the prison population's inexorable rise and a way to prevent reoffending, and which can operate as a continuance of any rehabilitative scheme inmates may have experienced whilst in prison. Any alternative must be cheaper, and anything ought to be more effective. Involvement in sport is one which this dissertation will consider in detail.

---

[33] Ainsworth, P., and Pease, K., 'Psychology in Action: Police Work' British Psychological Society, Leicester, London. Methuen. [1987]
[34] Re cost [for 2018] see note 24 [above]
[35] Currie, E., 'Confronting Crime' New York. Pantheon [1985]

The theory behind diversion is simply expressed but is a vastly complicated business to argue. Farrington[36] [at pp. 22-34] outlines the results of a long-term study of delinquency in the United States and in Great Britain and lists the factors which seem to set youths onto a path of crime and a recurring factor is that of the one-parent or broken-home. At page 28 he states:-

'One of the most successful delinquency prevention programmes has been the Perry pre-school project carried out by Schweinhart and Weikhart on disadvantaged black children ... to provide intellectual stimulation to increase cognitive ability [See Nichols[37] pp.185-186] *and to increase later-school achievement.'*

This was a two-year programme covering pre-school age children who attended a pre-school centre and backed up by weekly home-visits by the UK equivalent of the health-visitor network. At p. 29 Farringdon [ibid] at p. 29 mentions the Gendreau and Ross[38] programmes which aimed to modify the impulsive, egocentric thinking of delinquents to teach them to ...

' ... stop and think before acting, to consider the consequences of their behaviour, to conceptualise alternative ways of solving interpersonal problems. It included social skills training, lateral thinking, critical thinking, to value education, assertiveness training, negotiation skills, social perspective training, role-playing and modelling – demonstration and practice of effective and acceptable interpersonal behaviour ...'

In his conclusion, Farringdon [ibid] at p. 30 stated that ...

' ...Major efforts to tackle the roots of crime were needed especially

---

[36] Farrington, D., 'Early Developmental Prevention of Juvenile Delinquency' RSA Journal Vol 144, November [1994]

[37] Nichols, G., 'A consideration of Why Active Participation in Sport and Leisure Might Reduce Criminal Behaviour' Sport, Education and Society [1997].

[38] Gendereau, P., and Ross, R. R., '[Re]habilitation Through Education: A Cognitive Model for Corrections' Journal of Correctional Education [1979-89]

those focussing on early development ...' and ... 'The costs of the criminal justice system, viz., the police, courts, prisons, residential facilities for juveniles are so enormous in comparison to the cost of health visitors that bit would almost certainly be cost-effective to reallocate a proportion of the criminal justice budget to provide intensive health-visiting programmes for high-risk families ...'.

He agreed, too, that at a more general level, there is a need for the government to a switch resources from treatment into early prevention of crime and that the Home Secretary should announce a new programme of fundamental research into the causes and prevention of antisocial behaviour designed to lay the foundations for the reduction of crime and associated social problems in the next 20 to 30 years.

So far, we have considered that, whether people offend because they are a victim of circumstances or have some behavioural disfunction [see at 5 'The Offender'] it is in the public interest to bring about their reform, and wherever possible to prevent offending in the first place. We know that social and environmental influences which pull an individual towards delinquent behaviour can be diluted if not extinguished by early treatment [Farrington, ibid]. Success in diversion, a tangible and cost-effective benefit, will logically mean financial savings will be made on the cure aspect, e.g., prisons inter alia, which are doubtful in achieving their aims. Ought it be possible to rearrange the current cart and horse order?

3. Sport as Prevention

The phrase 'sport as prevention' is used to describe a wide range of approaches which can be characterised as 'the attempt to influence and control potential and actual manifestations of delinquent and antisocial behaviour by substituting sporting activities into young persons' behavioural repertoire. [Robins, p. 7]. Coalter [p.1] says 'The efficacy as sport as an antidote to delinquency is by no means settled.' Atherton [ibid, p.5] 'The use of adventure-based interventions for juvenile delinquents has received little attention from criminologists.' But Coalter makes it clear that the wide range of behaviour, both antisocial and delinquent, and the wide range of sporting activities made it very difficult to make any claims as to the benefits of sport, if such claims were not to be easily demolished. Nichols [p.81] 'There is little evidence for the effectiveness of such programmes in reducing crime.' Even in his 1999 paper[39] [at p.198] Nichols has little change of mind:-

'The rationale for projects that use sport and leisure experiences as a medium for counselling to change offending behaviour is underdeveloped. Projects are often justified by value judgements as a clear rationale that understands causal links between the experience of the project and the reduced offending.'

By contrast, the headline findings of the Sport England survey of 1999 [ibid] is more up-beat in its opinion :-

'... there is a growing body of evidence which shows that sport can make a significant contribution to individuals and to society ... many of those benefits - health, social regeneration and reductions in criminal behaviour - are not realised ... unless a positive attitude ... is developed at a young age ...'

It goes on to indicate that facilities and staff at many schools and facilities are, generally, are sadly lacking. The 'Best Value Through Sport' [ibid] in its foreword, responds to the challenge 'Why invest in sport?' as follows; 'This document draws on the best scientific

---

[39] Nichols, G., 'Is risk a valuable component of outdoor adventure programmes for young offenders undergoing drug rehabilitation?' The Journal of Youth Studies 2[1] 101 – 116 [1999]

evidence available ... it shows that for every pound invested in sport there are multiple returns of, for example, reduced criminal behaviour young people.' However, even within the 68 references given, it was impossible to establish the source of the scientific evidence.

Mid-Devon District Council[40] [MDDC] in their 'Youth Sports Development Strategy [2000 – 2003] was more circumspect. At page five they say that the Crime and Disorder Act of 1998 and the recent MORI survey [1999] of MDDC residents emphasise the importance and significance of sport to quality of life locally. And that sport increases self-esteem and can play a vital role in young persons' social amd moral development. It then reminds us [via a quote reproduced from NACRO[41] that young people can easily drift into offending behaviour through boredom and limited access to more constructive activities. The fuller explanation is as follows:-

'Levels of antisocial behaviour and criminal activity among young people are a major problem for society. The scale of youth crime is considerable. In 1996 it was estimated that seven million crimes were committed each year by 10 to 17 year-olds.[42] The causes of crime and disaffection among young people are complex and multi-dimensional. While it is unrealistic to claim that sport alone can reduce levels of youth crime in society, strong experimental evidence shows that sport can play a part in reducing crime and levels of antisocial behaviour in young people.'

4. The Evidence

4.1 Outdoor Adventure Programmes[43]

---

[40] MDDC Youth Sports Development Strategy' 2000 to 2003
[41] NACRO; Growing up on Housing Estates [1998]
[42] Office for National Statistics, HMG [1998]
[43] For a broad picture on programmes look at the Journal of Sport and Social issues – 'A Grounded Theory of Fitness Training and Sports Participation in Young Adult male

Juvenile crime comprises principally acts of commission; criminal damage, theft, minor assaults and taking cars. It does not need a behavioural psychologist to tell us that certain antisocial acts are born of boredom and whilst this lack of constructive occupation engenders a mental weariness, juveniles will turn their attention to seeking thrills. Doctor Barry Cripps, a sports psychologist, for the British Olympic Archery Team;

> *'Sport has a role in reducing crime. Kids left in the street will get into trouble. The nature of young people is that, if there is nothing to do, they will find something to do that is very often outside the law.'*

[Cited Jones[44] pp. 24 -25]

Roberts[45] at p.11 explains that :-

> *'... delinquency and all other riotous incidents can be exceptionally good fun for the perpetrators. Driving a stolen car is exhilarating ... pitched battles with the police can be particularly rousing ... there are really no socially acceptable alternatives that will deliver the same kicks ...'*

... though Roberts doubted that these perpetrators would be diverted by any socially-approved recreation. These pastimes also carry an element of risk, and it has been argued that it might be possible to replicate the risk element found in most illegal pursuits by engaging in lawful pastimes. The element of risk in canoeing and rock climbing has been examined within the context of young offenders undergoing drug rehabilitation [Nichols, 1999, ibid] and the conclusions to be drawn were that *'... as part of a long-term process, physical, emotional and social risks can be managed to achieve*

Offenders' Jan 2014. Retrieve from
https://journals.sagepub.com/doi/10.1177/0193723513520012
[44] Jones, V., 'match of the Day? Football and Crime Prevention'. Criminal Justice matters No. 23 Spring 1996
[45] Roberts, K., 'Leisure Responses to Urban Ills in Great Britain and Northern Ireland' in Leisure in the 1990s: Rolling back the Welfare State . Sugden, J., and Knox, C., [Eds] Eastbourne Leisure Studies Association [1992]

positive outcomes such as improved self-esteem, improved relations of trust ... and possibly a new interest that could lead to employment opportunities ...'

In support of this outcome, Rosenthal[46] at p. 61, when writing of Outward Bound experiences, concluded that physical activity involving risk is invigorating both physically and mentally and produces a state of well-being and elation, and when relating this to reoffending claimed an improvement on his programme over those who had not become involved in the Outward Bound scheme. However, little can be drawn from his conclusions as there could have been certain predispositions affecting the subjects and which impacted adversely on the credibility of the results; lack of credible control groups tends to dog much of this research.

The risk-theory and thrill-seeking may explain some crime, but it is a complicated debate encompassing acceptance / avoidance / enhancement of 'every-day' risk, e.g., crossing the road or smoking, to the deliberate generation of risk for reasons for reasons wholly related to the psychological make-up of the individuals concerned. Adams[47] sets out an interesting view of risk generally, and shows, inter alia, that risk is rarely an objective concept, as every individual has his ot her own ideas of what is risky and its degree, and weigh-up whether they are prepared to 'run it'. Within the concept of crime, especially youth crime, and antisocial behaviour, one has to ask whether the 'risk' associated with offending is synonymous with 'thrill' and whether

---

[46] Rosenthal, S. R., 'The Fear Factor; Sport and Leisure No. 23 [1982]
[47] Adams; J., 'Risky Business: the management of Risk and Uncertainty'. Adam Smith Institute, [1999]

lawful 'risky' activity can be an alternative.

One obvious disadvantage of following outdoor pursuit schemes as a stand-alone project in an offender programme is that they tend to be run over a comparatively short period, compared, say, to a pitch or court-sports programme which could extend over several months. Unless part of a more extensive rehabilitation exercise, for example to include a period of fitness training during which a close supervision can be undertaken of the subjects and how they cope, any benefit could be short-lived. Alternatively, it could be just one exercise of a more comprehensive package. Notwithstanding, it would be unfair to suggest that outdoor schemes do not have a place in reform. Atherton [ibid] at p.60 in his assessment of outdoor pursuits and young offenders concluded that :-

> '... Outdoor pursuits courses can be effective in rehabilitating young offender. Despite many methodological design faults, evaluation studies provide enough evidence to conclude that these interventions can have greater impact on recidivism than traditional justice sanctions ...'

But can they be effectively utilised to divert pre-deviants from offending? Risk can be experienced through conventional sports, and although not quite so extreme as the outdoor activities described by Atherton at p.1, it is to these and the benefits which may accrue therefrom which we now consider.

4.2 Sport; The Opportunities.

> 'Sport as prevention, is, on the whole, based on the belief that sport and recreation as a planned activity with juveniles can foster self-confidence, provide transferable skills, channel violence, provide opportunities for social interaction ... and

these goals parallel those of social and life skills training.' [Robins ibid, at p.7]

Physical fitness and sporting achievement may establish their self-identity via social relations [Trujillo[48] at pp. 162-173 and Hendry[49] et al], but do not our schoolchildren and young school-leavers have a good grounding in sport sufficient for them to have gained a real interest, and keen to follow on after school? To join clubs, improve performance, take further training and coaching? It is a good question but regrettably we seem to be sadly lacking in these aspects. The Young People and Sport National Survey [1999] on schools' sports programmes show that:-

The average number of sports done at least once in the school year was eight;

The average number of sports done at least ten times in a school year was four;

Only about half of primary-school children and 17% of secondary-school children participated in swimming on a frequent basis;

Only 33% of children spent two hours or more per week doing PT;

Only 68% of secondary-school children had access to a multi-purpose sports hall;

One third of secondary school teachers considered their sports facilities to be inadequate.

---

[48] Trujillo, C.M., 'The Effect of Weight-training and running exercise intervention programmes on the Self-esteem of College Women' International Journal of Sports Psychology
[49] Hendry, L.B, Shucklesmith, J., Love, J. G., Glendenning, A., 'Young People's Leisure and Lifestyles'. London, Routledge. [1993]

There are few if any areas of leisure which have such a pervasive impact on young peoples' lives as sport, whether they themselves play or watch their sporting heroes on TV. However, levels of involvement vary considerably between different groups in society. For many young people's participation in sport does not extend to their adult years where there are significant drops in the level of participation particularly in the early post-school years. Extracurricular opportunities are more accessible to middle-class families with flexible work arrangements and high levels of personal mobility.

The decline in PE in primary schools will mostly affect children from lass well-off backgrounds. These are the people who will be least likely to be able to take up the opportunities measured in years to come by increasing levels of vandalism and antisocial behaviour that a lifelong involvement in sport may have negated. [Young People and Sport National Survey ibid]. It is hard to imagine that things were any better in the past. A reasonable conclusion to draw from this is that those juveniles who do not excel at their academic work have had little opportunity to shine at sports as, quite simply, the facilities are poor and opportunities few. This is especially significant in view of the findings of Hendry, et al, [ibid] '... A considerable body of evidence supports the idea that an active leisure life can improve self-esteem ... leisure has a big part to play in helping young people to make healthy and successful adjustments in this phase of life ...'

In a Government Policy Statement of July 1995 'Sport – Raising the Standard', John Major, the then prime minister, is quoted as saying. 'My ambition is to put sport back at the heart of the weekly life in every school and to re-establish sport as one of the great pillars of education'. But we still have a shortage of sports facilities at schools and out of schools as they simply do not exist in many parts of the UK. In Paignton, Devon, it was reported that one primary school had to practice the 100 m. race on a street marked with bollards because of a shortage of sports facilities. [Savill[50]].

It is small wonder, then, that all the benefits which accrue to those who regularly participate are sadly denied to those who would participate but lack the wherewithal to access suitable facilities. This is reflected in the findings of Sport England, 'Best Value Through Sport' [1996] where the professional socio-economic group [Gp.1] were three times as likely to participate in sport as unskilled, manual socio-economic [Gp.3] and 16% of those in Gp.1 were members of sports clubs compared with less than 3% of Gp.3 and less than 5% of those in the semi-skilled manual group [Gp.2]. Regarding the use of local authority sports halls, 10% of visitors came from Gp.1 – 6% of the population as a whole – whilst only 8% from Gps.2 and 3 [19% of the population] made regular use of the facility. Clearly, the lower socio-economic groups are not well represented here. They do, however, feature more in the in the crime statistics; most people who commit crime come from working-class backgrounds [Rutter and Giller, 1983] though self-report studies indicate extensive delinquency amongst middle-classes, the majority of which is hidden. [Hood and Sparks[51]].

5. The Offender

It is significant that 70% of all prison inmates are suffering from personality disorders which does not necessarily mean that they are

---

[50] Savill, R., 'Pupils train for 100m sprint on town street' Daily Telegraph, 29 July [2001]
[51] Hood, R., and Sparks, R., 'Key Issues in Criminology'. Weidebfeld and Nicholson, London [1970]

suffering from a mental illness but that they lack, for example, interpersonal skills evidenced by, inter alia, difficulty in relating to other people. The majority will therefore benefit from treatment so one has to ask why they are in prison, and would they be there now if that had been exposed to early correcting influences? Rhetorical questions, but they do provoke thought.

We have seen through Farrington [ibid] that combinations of circumstances surrounding even quite young children may, if left undisturbed, affect them in such a way as to turn them to delinquent behaviour. These factors which are predictive of juvenile delinquency can be 'intercepted' although at they time probably inchoate and countered by the employment of certain skills first to recognise the conditions then to ameliorate them. It is worthwhile comparing the perceived benefits of sport with the deficiencies of juvenile delinquents with the idea of attempting to overcome the problems with a rehabilitative regime of properly developed sports activities for at-risk children and offenders.

Some commentators suggest that sports-related programmes can be tailored to suit individual deficiencies, but this is a degree of fine-tuning which would very probably require highly specialised analysis of individual characters. [Refer Coalter under 3 of this review [Sport as Prevention]]. This would be difficult to programme into team sports, would also be hard to monitor and would limit the free expression which most participants enjoy whilst playing sport. In any event, such a specialised programme would be more appropriate for a schedule for psychiatric patients. Notwithstanding, clients may have their own preferences which could be considered when working on their participation in any programme.

5.1 The offending Character

What is the psychological make-up of offenders and the at-risk juveniles which sports-based activities hope to divert to lawful activity? Ross and Fabiano[52] developed an understanding of criminal behaviour as 'being pre-disposed by a set of cognitive deficiencies' that were apparent in offenders. This included inability to solve interpersonal problems, to reason abstractly or to feel empathy with other people or to appreciate the need to comply with instructions, rules or laws. They manifested difficulties dealing with social relationships particularly with adults and showed a lack of self-control, a low locus of control, selfish and callous behaviour and paranoia. In summary, they showed the signs of just not fitting in with a regulated, law-abiding society.

It is not intended here to discuss in any depth the psychology of criminal conduct or to go into the favoured variables of age, race, sex or social class but rather to look at the benefits which can accrue or are said to accrue, through the medium of sport and overlay them with the deficiencies which affect juveniles and make them inclined towards offending behaviour.

Criminal and antisocial behaviour can be caused by momentary loss of self-control by an otherwise well-adjusted personality and may result in sexual or physical violence. In the Cambridge Study,

---

[52] Ross, R., and Fabiano, E., 'Time to Think; A Cognitive Model of Delinquency Prevention and Offender Rehabilitation' Ottawa T3 Associates Canada. [1985]

[Farrington, ibid] it appeared that convicted delinquents tended to be troublesome and dishonest in their primary schools, were aggressive and frequent liars at age 12 to 14, bullies by 14, antisocial at 18 in a variety of respects, and it is because of this versatility that measures likely to reduce delinquency will also succeed in reducing associated antisocial problems of sexual promiscuity, heavy drinking, substance abuse and gambling. [West and Farrington[53]].

Farrington [ibid]] also identified other factors which indicated the likelihood of delinquency which included impulsiveness and hyperactivity, lack of concentration, restlessness and daring at age 8 to m10, and low intelligence. Poor scholastic performance seemed to be prevalent among truants and those who left school at the earliest possible age without having passed any examinations. They generally do better at non-verbal tests such as object assembly and block design; i.e., find it easier to deal with concrete as opposed to abstract concepts. They also indicated a failure to foresee the consequences of their actions.

There was also a history of poor parental supervision, a lack of monitoring, product of large families with harsh nor erratic discipline and cruel or passive, neglecting parents, broken homes, family conflict and convicted parents, socio-economic deprivation. Adverse school factors arose where there was a high turnover in teachers and high truancy and delinquency rates and situational factors such as opportunities for crime, peer and parental responses. Aggression also tended to feature more prominently in the behaviour pattern of juvenile

---

[53] West, D.J., and Farrington, D. P., 'The Delinquent Way of Life' Cambridge Study in Delinquent Development' Harrington [1977]

offenders and also proved a good predictor. McMahon[54] at pp.344-351] opines that, although the causes are manifold, delinquent behaviour tends to be associated with depression and low self-esteem. It is this, amongst other things which sport may address.

5.2 Sport and the Offender

What can involvement in sport do to render ineffective in delinquents the inclination to offend? It is obviously not any physical barrier nor can it be any medical intervention [it could be in extreme circumstances, but this is outside the scope of this dissertation] so it must be some mental process which the client undergoes. But are they effective? McMahon found that vigorous aerobic exercises, with incarcerated delinquents] led to improved self-esteem and lowered levels of depression when compared with a control group. Regrettably, there was no information on whether there was any significant reduction in offending, understandable bearing in mind the group's circumstances. Recent US research [BBC Radio 4 programme; no further reference available] found that lying down in a darkened room for certain specified minimum periods can also reduce depression a d stress, so is this a case of the 'hop-on' culture by the sport's lobby, claiming that it is their method which produced the result?

Jones [ibid] states that the five benefits of participation in sport identified by Dallas Initiative for Diversion and Expedited Rehabilitation and Treatment [DIVERT] are increased self-esteem, improved relationships with peer group, productive use of time, the opening of new possibilities and the development of better

---

[54] McMahon, J. R., 'The Psychological Basis of Exercise and the Treatment of Delinquent Adolescents ' Sports medicine. [1990]

relationships with adults. Sugden and Yiannakis[55] [at pp.59-64] suggest that for some adolescents, delinquency provides one of the alternatives for developing feelings of mastery, competence, self-worth and a strong identity, which is, significantly, a selection of the sensations and emotions experienced by any competent sportsman. Sugden and Yiannakis added that the sports with the greatest rehabilitative potential are those with a de-emphasis on competition and externally-defined goals, but with a focus on personally constructed goals, a minimum of rules and small-group or individual activity.

Their analysis seems to support the idea that Outward Bound type exercises are more beneficial to the at-risk or delinquents with its concept of development training. One might argue that individual activity, unless part of a task set within the context of group activity, i.e., being responsible for executing a task upon which all the others will rely and which will form part of an overall objective, will be valueless because there will be no serious appraisal by peers and little emphasis placed on the 'society' of the activity.

One can forever sing the praises of sport, and it does have obvious benefits, but researchers will always come up against the inveterate problem of proof of its rehabilitative value. However, having re-established that, there are certain obvious benefits which accrue, and which can inhibit offending ability and opportunity. We have already seen that aerobic activity reduces depression etc., in nor out of prison or a YOI. Some are based on psychological factors; others are

---

[55] Sugden, J., and Yiannakis, A., 'Sport and Juvenile Delinquency ; A Theoretical Base.' [1982

common-sense, viz.,

Physical exertion is tiring and will naturally drain aggression, albeit for a period which depends on the scale of the exercise, the period over which the exercise is maintained and the circumstances and the environment;

Participation can isolate the client from his peer group as can any activity outside his normal environment and place him in a situation where his standard responses to other people and situations become unacceptable. His only option then would be total isolation or an amending of attitude, albeit temporary, again depending on circumstances;

Can foster a climate of interdependence between client and youth leader / instructor, a valuable opportunity to mitigate any damage caused by absent or poor parenting, a remedy more effective over a prolonged relationship;

Removes, albeit temporarily, and depending on circumstances, opportunity to offend;

Offers a chance to foster, in a constructive way, hitherto dormant leadership qualities and gives direction to, e.g., achieving something, whether team captainship, competition results or some level of competence where perhaps the client previously had no imagination or initiative;

Represents a challenge and meets any need for excitement.

Robins [ibid] gives examples which illustrate how initial shows of bravado and buffoonery on an Outward Bound course were ignored and those questionable talents channelled to more constructive effort as soon as those concerned realised the futility of their behaviour.

Another overcame her relative youth to show she was as good as her peers on the course. Atherton [ibid] at p.17 makes the point that there is little doubt that physical exercise has benefits and engenders feelings of well-being but what is less clear is whether it has any intrinsic, preventative or rehabilitative value. He adds that, ' ... even though sport may provide a temporary relief from boredom, young people could not play sport all day ...'. Why not? There is no reason why youths cannot spend many hours at some multi-purpose sports venue; they seemed otherwise content to hang around city centres all day achieving no positive result.

6. Crime Prevention Initiatives

6.1 Community Developments

Robins undertook an in-depth survey of several schemes established to, inter alia, attempt the diversion of 'at risk' juveniles and the reform of offenders. As he pointed out, many post-war estate developments which concentrated on affordable, terraced and semi-detached properties, long streets, poorly served with shops and community services, began to experience a pattern of youth behaviour spawned through hitherto repressed energy; having nowhere to let off steam, to play ball games, to ride bikes and generally behave in a way all growing kids do. The way their playful instinct manifested itself was a nuisance to immediate neighbours, their behaviour antisocial. It made the lives of some residents unbearable. Few of the residents were prepared to undertake any worthwhile measures to alleviate the problem. The town-planners had not accounted for the need. With instinct thwarted, this energy was diverted to make criminals of many. Car-crime, vandalism and violence was rife.

Enlightened authorities in the worst-served areas with virtually no dedicated sports grounds or facilities, but with a growing awareness of the enormity of the problem posed by the lack of facilities, began to act to head-off a disaster. NACRO via the National Safe Neighbourhoods Programme and the Government's Priority Estates Project and community-based organisations such as the North Kensington Amenity Trust[56] [NKAT 1971] began working on what they termed the 'estate based crime prevention projects' [Robins p.20]. Some practical issues had to be addressed when considering these initiatives. There had to be a degree of co-operation between local organisations who had control over, or access to, sports facilities. Professional or voluntary specialist sports workers also had to be available to work with at-risk youth.

Examples of these initiatives included BMX bike tracks, kickabout areas [Streethouse Estate, Wakefield, and in North Tyneside]. In an estate in Maidstone, the Mangravets, all they had initially was a patch of ground on which to play football. Better than nothing, but inadequate. In some inner-city areas, facilities included flood-lit playgrounds, all-weather pitches and sport and leisure centres.

The NKAT provided recreation areas, a covered sports pitch, a BMX track and a squash club. But there were difficulties; lack of parental supervision, lack of training in some disciplines and lack of finance. Many youngsters' ambitions were frustrated as there was a

---

[56] NKAT [now Westway Development Trust] was established in 1971. The Trust's remit was to improve the lives of the residents of the Royal Borough of Kensington & Chelsea. Westway Trust was given a long lease over 23 acres of land under the Westway (the Estate) where it passes through the Royal Borough. It is maintained for the benefit and enjoyment of everyone who lives and works in the Royal Borough of Kensington & Chelsea.

poor overall structure and a degree of peer pressure on many aspiring participants to disengage from the scheme. [Robins p.24].

A better track record is illustrated by Millwall Football Club Community Sports Development Scheme which has the backing of the club management and players and this is reflected by the fact that its sphere of influence has, with the approval of the courts, been extended to offenders referred to the club by the judges and magistrates and, generally, with the approval of the youth workers and probation services. Although to a degree, and erroneously, perceived as being an 'anti-football hooligan' initiative, its declared aims are to find ways to promote the good name of the club among local schools and youth organisations, to encourage family support of the club with the use of special facilities and to make those facilities available to youth groups and community associations, encourage involvement of young supporters in soccer and other sporting facilities. But football is the most popular sport for young people either as players or spectators, so it is little surprise that this initiative has met with success.

Some of the sports centres had, according to a Sports' Council report [1986] on their 'Sports for All initiative, little relevance to the requirements of inner-city youngsters. The facilities were primarily utilised then, as they are today, by the social classes who can most afford to use them and not by those who have a real need. In the report's own words, 'under-used by inner-city youth or taken over by social groups who already have a high sports participation ratio'. It goes on. Moss Side Leisure Centre, Manchester, another example, was subject to vandalism and theft, and a low-rate of usage due to its location[57]. Squash courts were under-used, expensive and inappropriate to the area. The Sobell Centre in north London[58], a wonderfully constructed and well-equipped centre was at one stage in danger of becoming a neighbourhood problem of its own, necessitating an exclusion policy against those who would or could have benefitted the most from its existence. Management problems and what appears to be some unwise policy decisions almost signalled its demise. User surveys indicate that it has moved very much towards the social scales reflected at Moss Side. At Mangravets, in Maidstone, Kent, the YMCA sports centre encountered exactly the same problems as Moss Side and Sobell, but seized the initiative in actively encouraging the lower classes by employing a youth worker in the YMCA centre with a brief to pursue outreach work among the Mangravet youth, the source of most of the disruption. Personal communication with Paul Morton-Kemp, a scheme manager [February 2001] reveals that they are still battling with appalling vandalism at one of their sites.

62. The Police Role

It is regrettable that many youngsters grow up in an environment thick with a deep mistrust if not hatred of the police, which is unfortunate as most police officers are decent, hard-working and dedicated, and, as Robins discovered during his research, there are many police-based initiatives which combine with schemes whose aims are diverting juveniles from antisocial and criminal activities.

---

[57] The centre is now thriving and has recently undergone extension programme and now coves three floors and 59,300sq ft. The leisure centre reopened in autumn 2018.
[58] Sobell Leisure Centre is situated in the heart of the London Borough of Islington. New management [Better] run the centre. It has an Extreme trampoline park, extended gym, improved changing rooms, boxing gym, junior gym, soft play area and Mind and Body Studio.

Surprisingly, some officers have made these initiatives an almost full-time occupation, some on permanent secondment from their principal areas of duty. Their enthusiasm, with police resources, court access and available facilities, has produced a worthwhile benefit to the at-risk and offending youngsters.

The Mangravets Estate is a football-based initiative operated by the community police officer with the aim of diverting youngsters from delinquent behaviour during the school holidays with a longer term aim of improving relations between police and public by working in a relaxed, non-confrontational situation to gain enhanced respect of the parents.

There is the Watford Football Friends, a summer holiday event organised by Hertfordshire Constabulary in association with the Watford football club. Its aims are to prevent crime, to enable youngsters to enjoy themselves at matches and other football based events, to sell community policing, and work with the Walsall Wood Police Amateur Boxing Club to 'foster better police / public relations whilst mindful of the need to improve relationships with the local youths thereby reducing crime and antisocial behaviour'.

These schemes appear to show better results overall than the larger operations referred to above and the interpretation of the data produced by Robins [pp.43–54] indicates that success is due to personal attention, the relationships between the youths and the officers, the setting of targets by way of games and matches and the local police service becoming closely involved with the subjects.

Knowledge of client history enables the police to 'put in a good word' where necessary as well as exercise influence over 'the lads' as a mentor or confessor.

The suspicions some participants might have regarding the police, that they are constantly under surveillance or possible breach of trust where a client might be a little too 'candid' about what he or his mates have been up to. Regarding that, PC Watson, of Walsall Boxing Club says '... I have said to one or two lads who tell me things, that they understand I will have to pass on this information, and the response has been, that is the reason they are telling me ...' That's not a breach of trust at all. [Robins p.51]

6.3 The Rehabilitation of Offenders

Essentially, there is little difference between programmes aimed at pre-offence juveniles and those targeting offenders termed in the latter case 'alternative to custody' cases. For the organisers, there arises a question of funding which compels the initiatives to link up with the probation services and other justice agencies to present a united front to the magistrates and judges, to alert them to the cost and other disadvantages of custodial sentences. As suggested in the Green Paper 'Tackling Offending' [1998] the probation service should 'aim to engender confidence in the sentences of non-custodial alternatives and to increase the options available for probation and community service orders.' The SSCP, one of the schemes studied, has been so successful that it has become part of the Hampshire Probation service. The organisers of the various schemes had a second hurdle to overcome as attendance and participation by offenders in some sport-related scheme is, or could be, directed under a Supervised

Activity Order, but the offender may militate against the obligation and Robins gives examples where the subjects have often been delivered to the training venues by their probation officers, or where others attend only sporadically and others attend but are so reluctant to participate that it is a waste of time for all concerned. Such behaviour is unfortunate for the offenders as they must be aware of the consequences, but it must also be a substantial burden on the organisers who need to show some degree of programme success for continued referrals and financial backing. That apart, the relaxed and open approach might make it difficult to get down to serious, structured training and programmes for matches and tournaments for those who are keen to make it work for them. [Robins p.60]

The stated aims of the Inner City Coaching Initiative [ICCI], a football-based scheme working in the high-crime area of Birmingham, are to 'encourage skill, fitness and improve social behaviour among young offenders.' It runs twice-weekly evening coaching sessions and is the initiative of one man, as many of these schemes are, and remains flexible in its policies to work around the inherent difficulties such schemes present. Another football-based scheme is the Chelmsford Juvenile Justice, which also operates a gymnasium and has a stock of outdoor adventure equipment. Then there is the Sherborne House Intensive Probation Programme and a scheme at Millwall which also works with at-risk youngsters; the DIVERT trust gives grants to projects aimed at young people who were offenders.

The Greater Manchester Probation Service Projects Unit is, even after fourteen years, still at basic staffing levels, and had no proper monitoring or evaluation of is work [Robins]. The latest information is that it is now defunct, and the Young Offender teams established under the Crime and Disorder Act appear to have taken over a section of its work [Personal communication, March 2001].

It is difficult to discover the characteristics of the demise of many of these schemes. Only the successful ones have readily-available information. There is always difficulty, even with the best run schemes, in drawing up statistics except where positive monitoring and follow-up work is undertaken. However, Jones [pp.24–25] concludes thus when considering football related projects:-

> 'No-one would argue that football is the sole answer to youth crime, but the continuation of such schemes is based on the assumption that a combination of factors will affect a young person's involvement in crime and that for some young persons involvement in playing football may be one of those factors.

6.4 A New Initiative

Bearing in mind the present uncertainty surrounding sports-based projects for social crime prevention, the Positive Futures initiative was opened in March 2000 by Mo Mowlem, Trevor Brooking, Lord Warner and Kevin Keegan as an act of faith. The scheme is a partnership between Sport England and the Youth Justice Board, and the UK Anti-Drugs Co-ordination Unit and its aims are to use sport as a way of reducing antisocial behaviour and crime and drug use within local neighbourhoods. Intended outcomes are a reduction in youth offending in the project locality, a reduction in drug abuse among 10 to 16 year-olds participating in the scheme and an increase in regular participation in sport and physical activity for the same age group. Initial funding was £950,000 of which HMG contributed £500,000 from assets confiscated from convicted criminals; the sum is disappointingly small when you bear in mind the the cost of building a new wall around Broadmoor prison is estimated at £29m.

Presently targeting 24 locations, the scheme has not been in existence long enough to note any trends in crime figures in the area of operation, but once figures become available both pro and anti-camps will look at them carefully. [Personal communication with Alan Jones, Youth Justice Board, May 2001]. Many existing schemes such as Youth Inclusion managed by the YJB and Sport England, will be brought into the first round of Positive Futures.

7. In-depth Review of Prevention Schemes

There are - and have been – many initiatives which purport to address the problems of youth crime, the majority in some way associated with sport, but there is a few factors which seem to guarantee a degree of success on a scale dependent on resources, personalities and dedication. Others just manage but on a small scale. By looking at two effective and large-scale programmes, it is possible to select indicators of success. It will be immediately apparent that the material [subjects] the programmes deal with are universal in character.

7.1 Solent Sports Counselling Project

7.1.1 General

Established in 1983 and born of a pilot sports project, the SSCP of the Hampshire Probation Service, now known as the Hampshire Probation Sports Counselling Scheme[59], had the benefit of extensive monitoring and been the subject of numerous reports and scrutiny and liaison with many criminal justice agencies. Virtually all of which have provided feedback; hence, the SSCP has a well-documented life. It was established as part of the National Demonstration Projects and the Sports Council Monitoring Team [Report 1990 - from which all the following information has been extracted] provides a substantial source of information illustrating its success in achieving its stated aim to '... develop an interest in sport amongst offenders and those considered to be at risk and aged 17 or over ...'

This was to be achieved via several objectives. To develop a programme of sport and leisure activities using resources throughout the area; to foster goodwill and co-operation of appropriate agencies; to reduce the rate of appearances in court; to foster the self-confidence of clients through achievement in sporting and leisure pursuits; to counsel clients in order to introduce them to sports and leisure activities in a friendly and sympathetic environment and to introduce and engender the integration of clients into established sports and leisure opportunities.

Over the period of the report there were 760 referrals mainly from the probation services from which number trends and effectiveness of policies can be established. The method of operation included a major emphasis on establishing an individual relationship with each client and arranging a suitable activity programme and counselling the client

---

[59] Best value through **sport** booklet - Toolkit **sport** for development is an excellent reference and covers Hampshire [see p.18 of the booklet]

in terms of his or her sporting performance and personal development. After an initial assessment, further assessments are carried out on a regular basis the frequency and depth of which depends on the client category with special interest taken of those most at risk. From each, an initial commitment was sought leading to self-assessment. The most difficult was weaning the client off the programme at the end of the agreed period, but this problem was to a degree mitigated by encouraging clients to maintain contact with the project staff and in particular with the key workers, the sports leaders, who were given individual responsibility for a client and with whom close working relationships were essential for the building of a good overall rapport.

Although during the first year of the project most of the work concerned involvement in sport, the sports leader also disseminated advice on appropriate topics related to his clients' affairs, such as job-finding. Other programmes were also instituted for personal hygiene, drug abuse, smoking and sex-education. Overall, personal contact and face-to-face work produced the best results as was found at the Southampton base, opened in 1987, and which changed its policy to ensure that valuable aspect - personal contact - was paramount in its relationships with clients.

Outward Bound activities also formed part of the project itinerary from which it was hoped clients would be able to benefit in several ways, socially, physically, psychologically and intellectually. Links were fostered with outside agencies to broaden the range of activities and social mixing. Work was undertaken with criminal justice agencies - such as bail hostels, assessment centres, remand homes, detention centres, prisons and juvenile justice units [JJU's].

7.1.2 Client Profile

Through the records maintained by the SSCP, those regarded as being 'at risk' make up most clients. 93% were male and of those two-thirds were aged between 17 and 21 years; of them, 85% were unemployed and 37% lived in board and lodging accommodation. Of 42 sample clients 45% had between one and three convictions, few had a criminal history beyond four years and the most common offences [in order] were:- miscellaneous [most, but not defined], shoplifting, stealing cars, burglary [homes], burglary [other than homes], public-order offences and, lastly assault. This is encouraging in a number of ways as it generally conforms to the national perspective and the offences are relatively minor; thirdly, many have a short history, and few go on to become career criminals. Being able to forecast behaviour patterns and backgrounds associated with criminal behaviour means more effective obstacles can be erected to deflect antisocial and criminal behaviour and more accurate targeting of 'at risk' groups by organisations concerned with reducing offending. A range of objectives established by the SSCP sports leaders, common to all clients and based on the overall profiles is regarded as the model to work for the best results. [Report, pp.21-32].

7.1.3 Success?

There are several conclusions in the last two reports on the project, one being that of another agency involved with the project :-

> *'It is evident ... that the concept of sports counselling is relevant to many client groups who, whilst not the subject of current Probation Orders, are clearly at risk. It is also clear that some of the smaller probation offices feel that their clients, too, would benefit from sports counselling being on*

hand locally.' [p.75].

The project director, in his introduction to his second annual report [1989] states that in his view '... the project is working well in meeting its aims and objectives ...' In the twelve-page conclusion to the final [1990] report the director writes that involvement with the project for many clients is ' ... a vital first-step in gaining the self-esteem and confidence to look for a job ...' And overall :-

> *'We believe the Solent Sports Counselling Project has done the groundwork for the probation service to play a significant role in sports development particularly amongst the young unemployed and for sports to play a major role in the mainstream work of the Probation service ... and the SSCP has proved that the probation service is the right agency to forge the necessary links with sporting organisations or the ultimate benefit of both parties and, of course, the offenders involved.'* [pp.86-87]

Perhaps a victim of its own success, the SSCP has now been absorbed into the Hampshire Probation Service so no longer exists as a separate entity. Whether the close association with the HPS will, in the eyes of the clients, detract from its value remains to be seen. Waldman[60] who has been associated with the project since its inception, talks of the 'befriending approach' whereby a worker can build a relationship of trust with the clients . He also points out that it is not the engagement in sporting activities alone which accounts for the success of the scheme.

7.2 A French Initiative

---

[60] Waldman, K., and Waldman, J., 'Whose sport?' Sports Counselling – the Hampshire Probation Scheme'. Criminal Justice Matters. No. 23 Spring [1996]

In contrast to the SSCP, the French solution was not based solely on sports-related activity but is relevant because of the number of factors common to the SSCP and which pointed towards success. The researcher Michael King[61], senior research fellow at Brunel University, is the source of much of the following information.

7.2.1 General

The French enterprise was born of a real concern by the government about steeply-rising crime-rates and nationwide unrest as a reaction to unemployment, added to a sudden realisation that, when millions of youngsters flood onto the streets with the schools breaking up for holidays, there were bound to be some who will inevitably relieve their boredom and vent their frustrations by engaging in criminal and antisocial behaviour. Spurred into action, and with an eye on the forthcoming elections, the Mitterrand government took two steps. The first was the immediate establishment of a programme of summer camps and activities for youngsters in towns and inner cities; secondly, the appointment of a number of commissions one to investigate the problems faced by young people in finding employment and the other chaired by Bonnemaison, entitled *'Opposing Crime – Prevention, Repression, Solidarity'*; its committee identified what it considered to be the principle causes of crime thus:-

> ' ... *living conditions and overpopulation; difficulties in integrating both social and in employment, changes in family life, disorganised social life during the day, absence of social controls in people's relations with one-another, poverty and exclusion of certain categories of the population from mainstream society ... drugs, alcoholism and economic crises ...*' [Bonnemaison[62] Report, p.31 cited King, 1987 p.4].

---

[61] King, M., 'How to make social crime prevention work – The French Experience.' Brunel University. NACRO [1987]

The report concluded that no single cause can, on its own, explain crime. Being a central government initiative, the enquiry demanded central government response. Although earlier reports had addressed this problem the Peyrefitte[63] Report, and whereas it had clearly identified the area, scope and reasons for crime, it failed to supply any worthwhile proposals for dealing with it. Bonnemaison's solution was to establish several partnerships at local, community and government level to oversee the implementation and running of various schemes to address the problems; they had the muscle, authority, finance and incentive. And it had to take the long-term view. Specific areas of action were targeted; social life, education, training, employment and social integration, courts and police, research and communication. [King, pp.3-4]

A diverse mix of projects was instigated and included work-experience schemes, job provision, college courses, establishment of youth centres, advice on job training, drug and solvent abuse, employment, accommodation and finance, school safety projects; the 'drifters' it engaged in more worthwhile pursuits such as theatre opportunities and in Lille it established a vehicle service-station for the sole purpose of youth training. Each province had a free hand in what it did to address the problems which it regarded as most pressing and knowing that it had the full support of not only the community, but also the government. The aim was to keep the clients busy, to supervise and educate them. Another recurring feature, as with most of these

---

[62] Bonnemaison, G., Chairman, 'Face a la delinquance: prevention, repression, solidarite.' Report to the Prime Minister from the commission des maires dur la securite, La Documentation Francais, Paris [1982]
[63] Peyrefitte, A., 'Response a la Violence – Rapport de la Comite d'etudes sur la Violence la Criminalite et la delinquance. Press Pocket. [1977]

schemes, is the emphasis placed on building relationships with a worker, in this case, the *educateurs* who were court and social workers and police officers seconded to summer projects. With clients of principally north African origins, *animateurs* were recruited to work with and to encourage those of a similar background to become involved in the various activities.

7.2.2 Client Profile

Although there were numerous initiatives organised at local levels, the target groups reflected many of the characteristic of SSCP clients. In Poissy, these were identified as the poor, the unemployed living in socially deprived areas, inadequate housing, large immigrant population a very high proportion of whom fell into the 12 to 25 age bracket, with rampant drug abuse and petty crime. In Villette, there was a very high proportion of under 25s from deprived backgrounds with high unemployment and lack of 'social opportunities'; in Lille there was bullying, unemployment, school-leavers with no qualifications, drug, alcohol and solvent abuse, begging, urban decay, multiple social problems, lack of self-discipline, poor literacy and numeracy skills. In addition, and featured generally throughout France, there was a problem with north African immigrants, involved with drugs and a high death-rate, illness and social isolation. In summary, the authorities were looking at school failure, unemployment, lack of prospects, identity crises, racism and marginalisation, idleness, personality problems and violence. Their problems were the same as those faced by most other western countries.

7.2.3 Success?

King [p.34] notes that there was an overall reduction in crime committed by young people, such as criminal damage, vehicle theft and assaults. He quotes supporting figures but reminds readers not to be deceived by this and fall into the 'positivist' trap' by ...

> ' ... measuring the effects of a major long-term initiative purely in terms of official crime statistics assuming that ... crime can be neatly isolated from mother forms of behaviour and that the changes in criminal statistics are necessarily caused by changes brought about by the new policy ...'

However, it would be doing an injustice to the programmes to ignore the steady decline in all major French cities during summer holidays year-on-year since the inception of the schemes, possibly due to engagement of the youth in summer camps or at other organised activities. Nor would it be fair to ignore the long-term aims of the programmes, of social integration, confidence-building and job acquisition and a reduction in crime. [King ibid]. Overall, King is upbeat in his assessment of the French programme, identifying the ills of French youth affecting other western countries but mindful of the possibility of programme establishments in it for the investment, status and security for their members. Notwithstanding, this does not, he adds, detract from the real achievements in terms of cohesion and cooperation towards the common end, the lowering of petty-crime rates. He suggests a ' ... series of planks with which to build a solid base ...' as a nebulous concept of social crime prevention ...'

> 'A clearly conceived youth policy; a policy of integration towards immigrant communities; a range of available activities; avoidance of criminal prosecution in juvenile crime; a wide policy of giving responsibility to young people and taking an analytical approach to crime prevention ...'

[King. pp.39-39]

8. Empirical Input

The author's experience of offenders has been gained by contact through attending various magistrates' and Crown courts, including the Old Bailey [The Central Criminal Court] when acting for his clients, defending them or pleading in mitigation after a guilty plea. His cases ranged from the most serious to the petty, from young to very old clients, male and female. Some prolonged investigations, sometimes over years, afforded him the opportunity to get to know some of his clients very well. Many of them, throughout the offending scale, seemed anxious to win approval and friendship of others, and targeted those whom they saw as their intellectual and social superiors on whom they sought a degree of dependence once removed from previously damaging environments. Juveniles in particular recognised, during frank discussions, that they did things, either criminal or plain stupid, because when with their peer groups they sought the group's approval, and by such gratuitous acts of vandalism, violence or shoplifting inter alia, and to which they cheerfully admitted, they wanted to build up their 'street cred' or sought to appear as a 'hard man' or earn some suitably evocative soubriquet, and in pursuit thereof rarely failed to rise to a dare which, even for them, was outside their comfort zone and which invited consequences far beyond that which they or their peers ever contemplated. It resulted in either criminal proceedings or serious injury, so displaying all the characteristics and behaviour patterns which came with attachment to an offending group.

What they learned, usually too late to recognise, was that only relatively few of their group indulged to the fullest extent in similar activity, the ones who regarded the antisocial / criminal / destructive behaviour of the others as entertaining, but had the sense to 'back-off' where they might themselves become involved, and a few of whom were unfortunately but unwittingly involved and then sanctioned as being part of a joint-enterprise incident. For his clients there was simply no other way to gain respect, which was in many cases because they lacked appreciation of available opportunities, or there were no opportunities at their local level, or born of a frustration stemming from lack of intelligence and most certainly from associating with a peer group most of whom were similarly lacking in social skills. In moments of introspection, however, they, or most of them, admitted to being keen to break away from the groups with whom they offended.

What they lacked was strength of character, a deficiency which could be addressed by a sport's mentor found in this approach to social crime prevention. Otherwise they displayed a short-termism, an ignorance of their personal circumstances, by which is meant their position on the social scale and intellectually, a lack of ambition or planning for their future and little awareness of the ultimate consequences of their behaviour. For juveniles, et al, who involved themselves in such personally-destructive behaviour, it was surprising that many also lacked sufficient confidence to approach any authority figure or organisation to investigate possible means of escaping when, in any lucid moments, they realised that their immediate future, on a day-to-day basis, or even longer term, that every day, almost every hour, they did nothing, went nowhere, planned nothing, unless it was either sanctioned by their peers or arranged by them. They were hopelessly and irredeemably locked into a situation which would only be terminated when they faced a life-changing episode such as serious injury or a spell in prison, either one of which would very probably worsen the individual's circumstances and dash any hope they ever had or might have had of taking a more constructive career path. A few harboured ambitions to join the Armed Forces, but those who floated the idea found no support from their peers, so abandoned the plan, or were themselves too apprehensive to enter the recruiting offices, or, when they started an on-line application, failed to continue with it by not responding to the e-mails they received from the recruiters. Others were 'knocked back' because they failed drug-testing, had some minor criminal convictions, were unfit or had too many 'inappropriate' tattoos, and admitted it was their previous 'lifestyle', such as it was, to blame for all or one of those fails.

Individuals within the offender's peer group were hitherto the only persons to whom they could relate, particularly when parents or carers took little or no interest in them or were too tied up in their own lives [drinking, drug abuse or hard-working single-parent families]. They were then left to buy attention as described supra and thereby scrapping their own lives by moments of silliness and continued to do so with disastrous consequences, and greater sanctions awaited those who failed to appreciate the gravity of their behaviour even after a minor collision with the forces of law and order.

When counselled in prisons or other institutions, it was evident that the situation was very much the same with obvious limitations. Young criminals will link up with others of similar psychological make-up, and it is the tenor of that liaison which may well determine the client's path on release. Two examples where clients [youths] paired up with, and in quite uncontrived ways and as a result of circumstances, with mature sensible inmates who influenced them to such a degree that they gained substantially from the relationship, exploited to the full the opportunities within the prison, and had every reason to expect not to return to their previous life once released. In both cases the relationships arose out of engagement in sport, in case one through badminton and the other from cross-country running. The prison had an excellent gymnasium and a running track around the internal perimeter of the prison. Had, the author says, his clients instead associated at the lower-end of the scale within the institution, then the stories might have been very different. Both youths stated that they valued greatly the restraining influences, the maturity, intelligence and guidance from their older mentors, and felt disinclined to let them down; they wanted to please. These examples are important because they illustrate the value of constructive, personal relationships as an influence in recovery. The obvious difference between engagement in sport outside and inside as in these cases, was that the parties were 'captive' and there were choices of activity including many sports, courses of education and reading. Too often, as the author researched this topic, he came to feel that prisons were just *depositories of wrecked lives - social inadequates, failures,* especially in view of the statistics which show the number of ex-prisoners who returned to jail so soon after release.

9. Conclusion

Re-addressing the question, 'Can active engagement in sport reduce criminal behaviour' and having read thus far, one can conclude that it probably can. There are many inter-playing factors which govern the early future of juveniles' involvement in offending behaviour, but many can be anticipated and with proper guidance avoided. If engagement in sport does successfully address many of the deficiencies found in the make-up of at-risk offending juveniles, then it reduces by a significant factor the likelihood of their offending / re-offending. This is the probable explanation of why those who do better at school, both in sports and academically, and go on to higher education are less likely to fit the offender profile, quite simply because they have less of a problem with self-esteem, have personal confidence and therefore feel no urge to seek membership of 'deviant' groups by themselves engaging in deviant behaviour. The other factors, inter alia, housing, large families, parenting, are all issues which are, or should be, picked up and dealt with just as with the US experiment. [See under 2 supra].

With at-risk and offending juveniles, it is probably not sport per se that offers a chance of reform but as a raft which carries the clients into a physical environment, into an ambiance in which they feel more able to express themselves and can 'open up' and relate to their new peers. The important thing is that the clients can work with a youth-leader, instructor or some other adult without the 'metaphorical' desk dividing their respective 'worlds' where it would be almost impossible to build up a relationship of trust wherein the client begins to deal with the misconceptions he may have viz-a-viz himself and the rest of society and which will begin the readjustment process. It will, in addition and hopefully, ease him away from the individuals who were hitherto his entire 'world' and who would, or could, ultimately ensure his descent into antisocial and criminal behaviour.

An environment in which an appropriate relationship flourishes could never exist when the mentor figure by situation, dress, or authority, cannot identify with the client enough to encourage the client to please and to work with that figure. Indeed, Waldman [p.28] makes this point exactly:-

> 'Many of the SSCP participants will be very used to relating to professionals in formal settings and with formal agendas, the very situations at which they feel ill at ease. The scheme staff member will be alongside, and it is the interpersonal relationships ... that is the key to this scheme. The sporting focus is only half the sum ...'

On the sports field just as on the Outward Bound courses, there is a breaking-down of all these barriers; it becomes a more intimate environment which fosters the *milieu* in which a relationship will grow, where the client wants to be accepted, wants to please and to begin to construct his own world not be a hostage to impulse or to the whim of others or to wherever he will drift from day-to-day. He is encouraged to strike-out on his own for an independence, away from the influence of a delinquent group with its immediacy, it's short-termism and meandering existence. Of the more successful programmes several characteristics seem universal. The prerequisite for success appears to be the inclusion of most of these features but certainly the mentor figure is an absolute essential. To replace it or remove it is to construct that desk and the formality so destructive of the relationship. Programmes will include:-

> Ancillary activities, i.e., talks, job-search schemes; provision of suitable venues, open-early, close-late all day and every day; suitably qualified staff; mentor allocated to each client; proper assessment procedures; engagement in activities of new peer groups to exclude old associates; informal engagements with programme staff; long-term programming; opportunities for clients to improve performance, setting of attainable targets; an 'open house' to

permit 'graduates' to maintain links with staff.

They will have to be appropriate, of worthwhile length, flexible. The more successful ones will contain provision for all the above. Sport is an essential ingredient but only as it happens [currently] to be the most convenient medium and can encompass all these essentials which cannot exist independent of that foundation, as they will simply not work in isolation. Sport is a medium with which everyone can identify. It comes with its own rules, it has variety, can be simply located and requires no specialist knowledge. Indeed, other schemes such as in France, may be equally successful in achieving their aims but the diverse projects, essential to engage the attention of the clients own diverse interests, detract from the simplicity so adding to the costs and organisational complications.

Unfortunately, not all the schemes described show that they offer an effective regime in achieving their objectives. Robins cites examples where many have failed. Some took a short-term approach; some were under-funded or undermanned with one or two dedicated staff doing a good deal of work but against impossible odds. Management in others left a lot to be desired and the centres had often been vandalised. There is need for these schemes; they are not easy to operate without proper funding and community acceptance of their value. As with the French solution and the SSCP they have to be long-term projects. The government has a major role to play and it should heed the words of Farrington when he urged the government to switch resources from treatment to prevention but will they? John Sheppard, a charted psychologist, made the point at the end of the Farrington lecture that it is rewarding for a Home Secretary to focus on a cure as he can be seen to be doing something, whereas prevention is not seen to be doing anything at all so there is no political reward. As the writer so often says, with many politicians, it is *self* not *society* which is at the top of too many politicians' agendas. Farrington agreed that there is no immediate pay-off within the tenure of a Home Secretary, so little pressure to embark on any of these projects.

The appalling murder in Wales[64] by four people, three male, one female, in June of 2000 exposed the very worst of inner-city decay and societal neglect found in some inner-housing estates. There are many layers between the law-abiding caring elements of communities who cause little concern and the very lowest as illustrated by that case and worthy of constant scrutiny by all elements of authority but which is rarely afforded them until it is too late. Anne Widdecombe, the then shadow Home Secretary, in a June 2001 speech made whilst visiting a similar London estate, accepted unequivocally that such an environment was conducive to criminal activity; would she respond, if in power with the hammer of punishment when such activity arose or would she use the spanner of prevention to repair, by addressing and rectification of the deviant inclinations such circumstances engendered?

Until the murder, every authority displayed a reactive mind-set, but proactive intervention might have frustrated the inevitable consequences of ignoring the urban decay which nurtured all that was bad about social degeneration which does little to excite ambition, family values, self-esteem or a thirst for learning and self-improvement. It would be disingenuous to suggest that a balance is

---

[64] Mandy Powers, her two daughters, and her mother were all beaten to death.

easily found but arguably a neglect to not try to find one.

In Lancashire recently a successful youth club and spots centre had its local authority funding withdrawn because the authority subsidy ran at £5.00 for every £1.00 paid by members of the facility. These examples may be illustrative of, in the first case, ignoring severe social neglect and in the second skewed thinking dictated by accountants led by a *'price of everything, and value of nothing'* culture.

Childhood tendencies towards offending behaviour can be diverted by early intervention. We appreciate that therapy can, to a greater or lesser, extent mitigate behaviour brought on by personality disorders; we know that to occupy otherwise idle hands in legitimate activity will discourage destructive, youthful exuberance. We can argue that engagement with the courts, YOIs and prisons can exacerbate problems and that reconviction rates are high, and prisons rarely deter. Most important of all, common sense dictates that prevention is better that cure.

Whether or not sport is the preventative, it ought to be given a chance and is a better option that just ignoring the problem or providing cures. At the very least this review suggests that sport deserves a chance, and its exponents given a fair hearing on how it can perform the task of crime prevention.

Deficiencies shown by the pre-deviant character of at-risk juveniles and in post-deviant youth are susceptible to the benefits of a form of social integration via a personal relationship which may be available through a sport-based programme. With the rising cost of attempting to cure crime, the doubtful efficiency of the various methods by which this is attempted, we should be working towards the *'dividend of prevention'* and whereas sport may be the solution, comprehensive research backed by the resources available to central government is needed if a definitive answer is to be found.

The answer to the question *'Can Active Engagement in Sport Reduce Criminal Behaviour'* is ... *'Probably'*. If it could be offered with education to a decent level, then it would be more definite than just a probable.

Bibliography

Adams; J., 'Risky Business: the management of Risk and the Uncertainty '. Adam Smith Institute, [1999]

Ainsworth, P., and Pease, K., 'Psychology in Action: Police Work' British Psychological Society, Leicester, London. Methuen. [1987]

Association of Chief Officers of Probation, January 2000

Atherton, J., Outdoor Pursuits Courses and Young Offenders. University of Cambridge. Unpublished dissertation for award of MPhil., Criminology. [1994]

Becker, H.S., Outsiders: Studies in the Sociology of Deviance. London. [1963]

Bonnemaison, G., Chairman, 'Face a la delinquance: prevention, repression, solidarite.' Report to the Prime Minister from the commission des maires dur la securite, La Documentation Francais, Paris [1982]

Butcher, J., R., 'Jail Education' Telegraph 22 December 1997

Braithwaite, J; Crime, Shame and Reintegration. Cambridge University Press. [1989]

Carey; G, Archbishop of Canterbury, also attacked Howard's policy on crowded jails in a Daily Telegraph article [8 April 1995].

Cavadino, M., and Dignan, J., 'The Penal System: An introduction. London, Sage [1997]

Coalter, F., Sport and Antisocial Behaviour; a policy review. Research Digest no. 41 The Scottish Sports Council, Edinburgh [1996]

Currie, E., 'Confronting Crime' New York. Pantheon [1985]

Daily Telegraph, January 29th, 1998, anon]. In 1996 the figure for new prison construction was £1bn. The cost of running the prisons already commissioned [2001] rises by £1bn per month.

Farrington, D., 'Early Developmental Prevention of Juvenile Delinquency' RSA Journal Vol 144, November [1994]

Gelsthorpe, L. R. Diversion in English and Dutch Juvenile Justice in Fennell, P.,

Gendereau, P., and Ross, R. R., '[Re]habilitation Through Education: A Cognitive Model for Corrections' Journal of Correctional Education [1979-89]

Gilling, D., Crime Prevention Theory, Policy and Politics. University College London Press. [1997]

Harding, C., Jorg, N., and Swart, B., [Eds] The Europeanisation of Criminal Justice. OUP[1994]

HMSO A Digest of Information on the Criminal Justice System. HMSO London [1991]

HMSO Statistical Bulletin 5/97 'Reconviction of Prisoners, England and Wales. London [1997]

Hargreaves, J; Sport, Power and Culture. Cambridge University Press [1986]

Hendry, L.B, Shucklesmith, J., Love, J. G., Glendenning, A., 'Young People's Leisure and Lifestyles'. London, Routledge. [1993]

Hood, R., and Sparks, R., 'Key Issues in Criminology'. Weidebfeld and Nicholson, London [1970]

Jones, V., 'match of the Day? Football and Crime Prevention'. Criminal Justice matters No. 23 Spring 1996

Jupp, V., 1 'Sport and Society'. Criminal Justice Matters No. 23, 1996 pp 24 & 25]

King, M., 'How to make social crime prevention work – The French Experience.' Brunel University. NACRO [1987]

Mayhew, P; Elliot, D and Dowd, The British Crime Survey HMSO [1989]

MDDC Youth Sports Development Strategy' 2000 to 2003

McMahon, J. R., 'The Psychological Basis of Exercise and the Treatment of Delinquent Adolescents ' Sports medicine. [1990] NACRO; 'Growing up on Housing Estates' [1998]

Newburn, T; Youth Crime and Justice; Young People and Crime . Oxford handbook of Criminology . Maguire, M, Morgan, R and Reiner, R [Eds] OUP [1997]

Nichols, G., 'A consideration of Why Active Participation in Sport and Leisure Might Reduce Criminal Behaviour' Sport, Education and Society [1997].

Nichols, G., 'Is risk a valuable component of outdoor adventure programmes for young offenders undergoing drug rehabilitation?' The Journal of Youth Studies 2[1] 101 – 116 [1999]

ONS Office for National Statistics, HMG [1998]

Peyrefitte, A., 'Response a la Violence – Rapport de la Comite d'etudes sur la Violence la Criminalite et la delinquance. Press Pocket. [1977]

Ramsbotham, Sir David, Chief Inspector of Prisons [March 2000]

Roberts, K., 'Leisure Responses to Urban Ills in Great Britain and Northern Ireland' in Leisure in the 1990s: Rolling back the Welfare State . Sugden, J., and Knox, C., [Eds] Eastbourne Leisure Studies Association [1992]

Robins, D; Sport as Prevention; The Role of Sport in Crime Prevention; Programmes Aimed at Young People . Centre for Criminological Research, University of Oxford [1990]

Rosenthal, S. R., 'The Fear Factor; Sport and Leisure No. 23 [1982]

Ross, R., and Fabiano, E., 'Time to Think; A Cognitive Model of Delinquency Prevention and Offender Rehabilitation' Ottawa T3 Associates Canada. [1985]

Rutter, M and Giller, H; Juvenile Delinquency; Trends and Perspectives , London, Penguin Books [1893] .

Savill, R., 'Pupils train for 100m sprint on town street' Daily Telegraph,29 July [2001]

Sport England. Best value through Sport; the value of sport . London. [1999]

Sugden, J., and Yiannakis, A., 'Sport and Juvenile Delinquency ; A Theoretical Base.' [1982]

Sunday Telegraph, 21 November 1999 [anon] Criminals set to be denied council homes' headline.

Tame, C. R., 'Freedom, Responsibility and Justice; The Criminology of the New Right' in Stenson, k., and Cowell, D., [Eds] 'The Politics of Crime Control. London. Sage [1991]

Tilt, R., 'Reformation lies in jail education' Telegraph, 22 December 1997

Trujillo, C.M., 'The Effect of Weight-training and running exercise intervention programmes on the Self-esteem of College Women' International Journal of Sports Psychology

Waldman, K., and Waldman, J., 'Whose sport?' Sports Counselling – the Hampshire Probation Scheme'. Criminal Justice Matters. No. 23 Spring [1996]

West, D.J., and Farrington, D. P., 'The Delinquent Way of Life' Cambridge Study in Delinquent Development' Harrington [1977]

Wilkinson, J; British Journal of Social Work; Using a reconviction predictor to make sense of reconviction rates in the probation service. 24[4] pp 461-475 [1994]

Letter to Michael Gove

12 October 2015

FAO : Amy Hawkes

[CC : Rebecca Pow MP]

I refer to our earlier contact and [again] to the letter of 3rd September from Michael Gove MP sent to Rebecca Pow MP, and which I received on the 29th inst.; I attach a copy for your convenience.

Bearing in mind the speed at which prison reform proposals are hitting the headlines today, and on which I also have an opinion, I thought best to get my ideas to the table sooner rather than later.

Hence, a somewhat truncated version of the brief I had originally planned.

I trust you will find it useful.

Cochrane.

Brief CV

On retiring from HM Forces, I qualified and worked as a lawyer for nearly 40 years. I have spent many hours at the Old Bailey and in dozens of Crown Courts and in almost every case came away with the impression that a great deal of time, money and resources were being wasted. And that locking people away is not the best way to deal with offenders unless something meaningful could come of it; it rarely does.

I have a master's degree in criminology and another in Research [HM Forces Summary Justice] and a Certificate in Education in the Development of Learning, Post Compulsory Education] and a Certificate in Counselling Skills. Part of my training was spent teaching prisoners and adults with learning difficulties.

I also lecture in law as part of my work.

There are many issues which lend themselves to scrutiny when one addresses the prison service. However, I have covered only a few of the more pressing matters.
I hope you find this missive of some interest.

Some notes on prison reform

1. <u>2. / PRISON NUMBERS</u>

In comparison to other European countries, we have a very high proportion of our citizens in jail. This statistic should not be a consideration in UK prison reform. We sentence individuals according to our principles and our way of life, and we should not act to please any other nation. What other countries do is their business, but that is no reason why we should not learn from them.

To engage in meaningful reform of the prison system we have to dump the existing model and current thinking on sentencing policy; some essential reform may be unpalatable but whatever is done has to be fair to the injured parties and to the offenders. However, the main issue is cost, not politics. To spend as much as we do on looking after the bad men in society when we have serious problems affording health care, schooling and defence, is anathema to the general public; this is understandable.

We cannot build more prisons as we did over the 16 years from 1980 when, to deal with overcrowding, twenty-one new prisons were built or altered to provide nearly 20,000 new places. This proved inadequate, and further proposals were considered for the 21st century to bring the total number of prison places up to 70,000; currently we have just shy of 86,000 people in prison. Clearly there is a problem.

Whatever changes are muted regarding the criminal justice system, there is one issue which deserves serious consideration and about which there can be little argument; building and maintaining prisons is hugely expensive and we simply cannot afford to build our way out of the overcrowding problem or, as has happened in the past, not send people to prison, even though they might have deserved it, just because there are no places available.

To hand-down a non-custodial sentence on some 'prison-bound' offenders merely because prisons are full was grossly unfair on those convicted criminals who were jailed, and it begs the question – was a prison sentence essential in those cases ... or wasn't it?

If our judges are not minded to restrain their use of prison as punishment then sentencing should become the prerogative of a 'Sentencing Panel', which, apart from cutting out the many apparently inexplicable and patently weird anomalies in judge-sentencing we read of today, it will produce a more balanced result with every aspect of the defendant's life, past record, inter alia, properly considered. If judges are reluctant to accept any fettering of their sentencing powers, as they always are, then legislation may be necessary.

A prison sentence for a first-time offender should not be applied except in cases involving violence, use of weapons and other cases where a person was killed or seriously injured and where protection of the public from these offenders is paramount. For white-collar crime, other sanctions should be applied [see infra].

We must fix the number of prison places, as imprisonment cannot be imposed regardless of cost nor should we suppose that our prisons will be full for the foreseeable future as, to do so, means our law and order services [and very probably our education system] are failing, and, were we successful in reducing crime, we cannot maintain empty prison cells.

Fixing the number of places should be calculated by looking at the number of spaces currently available [excluding 'spare capacity'] in the prisons we want to maintain – e.g., discounting the prisons scheduled for closure.

Several issues arise if we set a maximum number; firstly, we will have a situation where we will initially have more people in custody than a negotiated maximum. To deal with this there should be a policy over a period - say two years 'the run-down period' - of releasing the number of inmates who are next due for release such that at the end of the period the prisons hold only the number they were built to accommodate, and in that programme take account of the number of places lost by prison closure with their inmates being moved to the remaining prisons. This is a simple exercise in mathematics.

Statistics produced in late 1996 show that approximately 100,000 individuals were committed to prison or young offender institutions over each twelve-month period; then the prison population was roughly 53,000.

These figures are ten years old, but there is no reason to suppose that the proportions differ markedly from those of today. At least it gives a starting point and indicates that maybe half of all prisoners will be at - or very close to - their earliest date of release or certainly within one year.
Most custodial 'experiences' are very short, with the overwhelming majority in prison for days, weeks [ridiculous !] or months rather than years. [Refer Annual Prison Statistics]

Using up-to-date figures of the annual turnover of prisoners and the number in jail, will permit a reasonably accurate shot at how many have one year or less left to serve of their sentences.

What we need to achieve here is how many prisoners can be released over the assumed two-year run-down period without releasing any prisoners who still have a substantial period to serve, as this will be unacceptable for the public and too easy for the offenders.

There will also be a need to accommodate remand prisoners who will, more than likely, be ultimately sentenced to a term in prison.

Once settled down, a prisoner 'exchange' system will operate; new prisoner in, and the prisoner or prisoners next due for release, out, so there should never be any overcrowding. With this in place, and a serious review of the use and effectiveness of prison, the prison population should fall dramatically.

The repatriation of non-UK domicile prisoners should be considered as a major factor in reducing prison numbers. The Prime Minister is addressing this problem and the press suggests that by shipping 300 prisoners to Jamaica we will save £10m p.a., about £34,000 per prisoner; this is not a bad average, as ten or so years ago, expenditure was about £28,350 per prisoner.

Prison Statistics England and Wales shows the high number of foreign nationals in our prisons, so, if repatriation can be affected, although for various reasons not always possible, it can represent substantial savings.

Unfortunately, this is more than just a mechanical process, as doubtless the politics of the recipient countries will intervene but, notwithstanding, is a policy which should be vigorously pursued.

2. SHORT SENTENCES

Short prison sentences - less than one year - are counter-productive. They do not 'work' to achieve the aims of the prison service. For the short-stayer, the most significant aspect is his loss of liberty, but he will soon appreciate that he is being accommodated, fed, clothed, has access to health and dental care, sports facilities, TV.

And he will have contact with his family.

It is all free. He does not have to take exercise and he can choose to work or not to work. He does not have to take any course of education. In fact, short-term prisoners are not usually welcomed by the education department, as there is insufficient time for either side to get anything positive from it, or for the educators to find a suitable course of instruction for him. They are, rather, a bit of a liability, taking up time and space which could be afforded the long-term inmates who may want to achieve some qualification. Nor is there time for him to engage in any other rehabilitation programme.

However, drug addicts must be clean before they leave prison and if thereafter, they refuse treatment, then they should be returned to prison; drug addiction is at the root of many crimes.

Our short-term inmate does not therefore 'properly prepare for his return to society'; he leaves as he goes in, but with one difference; he now knows prison is easy; he no longer fears another 'stretch'. Prison as a deterrent will no longer work.

Short sentences are therefore pointless and an expensive waste of prison places and resources. Alternatives to jail must be considered in these cases, and, as mooted above, re-jig sentencing policy and educate the judiciary into not handing down short custodial sentences where, if a little more thought were applied, a non-custodial sentence would do.

[As an aside, many prisoners who do engage in meaningful education programmes, when moved to a different jail often find that their education records do not follow; this is an administration issue and is utterly wrong].

The application of a little common-sense should be applied. In one case, a minor drugs offender, a foreign national, was sentenced to nine months in jail. All he wanted to do was to get home, and it was difficult to understand why he was not just given a ticket and sent packing, but with immigration being notified that he was never to be allowed back into the UK.

Such situations as this occur time and time again, at vast cost to the taxpayer.

3. PURPOSE OF PRISON

Prison has many stated purposes. The high rate of repeat offending indicates that prison does not work; why not? A sensible view is that it is too easy, as alluded to above. There are too many facilities available to the inmates and which makes their lives too comfortable.

Tighter control should be exercised to prevent drugs and mobile 'phones being smuggled into prisons.

Prison should be a course, a regime of compulsory education and exercise through which prisoners should earn their release; a pass is freedom, there are no failures. There are many highly-qualified professionals and craftsmen in prison, whose services can be utilised by the prison service to train and educate.

On release, a prisoner should be encouraged to work for his living; a job [as well as finding a partner] is a good start in reducing re-offending, and starting his own, legitimate, business should be one target for the education and training he can receive in prison.

If we are to assist offenders to settle into life on the outside, they must be given a chance; they should be given every credit for staying out of trouble for the years it takes for his conviction to be 'spent' when he is, in the eyes of the law, 'reformed' and therefore entitled to be treated as every other citizen and not have his past dragged up at from time to time when he ventures from the shadows. Currently, a conviction is like a tattoo; it is there, somewhere, for life, which is not at all helpful for those who are genuinely reformed. Once a conviction is 'spent' it should be erased from all records.

4. THE COST OF IMPRISONMENT

Prisoners should pay for their board and lodging; the parents of young offenders could be asked to contribute.

A tariff can be set for each category of prisoner, the prisoner's means and the length of the sentence.

Recovering say, a mere £1.00 per day, either from his pay or from outside sources, from 87,000 prisoners would mean £30m per annum, collection cost excepted.

This can hardly be regarded as unreasonable when we have elderly people in care who are liable to have all but some £23,500 of their estates seized to pay for their care, and many homes are sold every year to raise the money. Or when a person, a normal law-abiding citizen, is pursued for debt, everything he owns can be attached by the creditors to settle the account.

Why should a convict be allowed to hold onto his realty, personalty and bank accounts either at home or abroad, when the state pays up to £30,000 p.a. to keep him in prison ?

Admittedly, there will be some who will genuinely have nothing, so the state should therefore consider other available options.

Assets owned by the prisoner will be liable to confiscation and whether the proceeds of crime or not. On release, any shortfall can be recovered from any future benefit payments, or a lighter tariff if from earned income. Prison would be a less attractive option if the prisoners were made to contribute to the cost of their keep.

5. PRISONER PROFILE

Perverse as it may sound, there are some decent people in prison. People who should not be there, people who have led blameless lives for 20, 30 or 40 years as adults but for which no credit is given when it comes to sentencing.

People whose lives are ruined anyway as a result of their crime and who are doubly-punished by losing their livelihoods, and whose whole family suffers.

Why therefore, when a woman is spared prison because she might have young children, the same should not apply to the family bread-winner, whose absence from home for even six months could will devastate the family, maybe mean the loss of the family home?

At least, while still living in the community, and no doubt lost his job especially as a professional person, he will be able to start immediately re-building his life; a person who will never in a million years be convicted of any other offence.

Consider the prisoner profile; generally, socially and economically disadvantaged; manual or unskilled worker if at work at all; fewer than ten percent with any qualification beyond 'O' level; rented or no accommodation; most left school before the age of 16 [refer supra – the mention of a poor education].
The point; is not a custodial sentence grossly unfair with the individual whose profile is far removed from the average, and with the almost inevitable loss of status and job, when he loses considerably more that the 'normal' prisoner who has virtually nothing else to lose anyway?

Understandably, the gravity of the offence will be a factor, but the old arguments 'You of all people should have known better' or the 'gross breach of trust' or 'you are an educated man and should have known better' must surely be dumped bearing in mind the far-reaching consequences of his actions.

We trust airline pilots to keep us safe; we trust builders with our property and accountants to look after our money, garages to ensure our cars are safe to drive. Those ex-offenders, professional or otherwise and who really care about themselves and their families will have their 'history' available on the internet 10, 20, 30 or more years later, so seriously jeopardise any effective rehabilitation.

Another category of prisoner also deserves special consideration; former members of the Armed Forces. [Matthew Green's book **'Aftershock'** [Portobello £20.00] should be compulsory reading on this topic].

This may be a matter which required the co-operation of the MOD, but our guys, many who joined up whilst still teenagers, may leave after serving their terms, and find it very hard to settle into civilian life. When the camp gates close behind them, they are suddenly alone with a holdall; their friends, their boss, left behind; their whole way of life ends there. They move from a family where everything has been done for them, and it is little wonder that they cannot cope. They are shown no favours; in fact, sometimes, the very opposite; nobody wants them. Many have no transferable skills; they start from the bottom.

Recent events mean many leave the forces very disturbed [PTSD] and / or severely maimed and it is a scandal that [a] they have to rely on charity and [b] get no meaningful on-going support as for example the VETS do in the USA. No surprise, therefore, when many of them finish up on the streets, and to ignore the difficulties they face will mean more and more of them will almost inevitably end up engaging with the criminal justice system – a short move from there to prison.

MPs whose constituencies include service establishments are very probably aware of this problem. It might help if [a] the resettlement period were extended to at least a full year full-time and [b] where higher and university education were free and [c] they and their families went to the top of the list for local authority housing.

Forces personnel deserve nothing less bearing in mind what they were prepared to do for us. Many of these guys find it hard enough to live with what they have seen and done in their service careers and cannot be expected to just suddenly become a 'civilian'.

Read Matthew Green's book.

6. **SUMMARY**

Fix the number of prison places;

Re-think on short sentences;

Apart from in exceptional circumstances, no prison for first offenders;

Make inmates pay for their time in prison;

Accent on education and exercise;

Train and assist prisoners so they can set up businesses on release;

In rehabilitating offenders, remove all internet references once the Rehabilitation of Offenders' Act deems the offence 'spent' Once spent, it should be spent for every purpose, including later convictions;

Look carefully at ex-forces personnel in prison; engage with the MOD to ensure they are given every assistance to re-integrate.

Researcher's collected essays to Police and Criminal Justice Studies. Period 1999 to 2001.

Essay 1: The Penal Process.

It is more than likely that any open-minded enquirer into the effectiveness of custody in the criminal justice system in meeting its stated objectives will conclude that the public are not getting a good deal and, mindful of the exorbitant cost of maintaining these places of detention, may recommend a long-overdue and serious appraisal of the whole concept of imprisonment. This would reflect the general opinion of most commentators. But law and order are hot political topics and one on which politicians can manoeuvre for, the cynic might suggest, less to deal effectively with a pressing issue and more to gain votes or the approbation of the public; it is one where our enquirer will see government policy closely following the crow. But is the crown blissfully unaware of the reality of the situation? Very probably it is. It was perhaps with his mind on votes, or maybe he was genuinely lost for any alternative remedy to the malady that was a climbing crime-rate, that the former Home Secretary Michael Howard in 1993 came up with his oft-repeated 'prison works' maxim.

Either way, it is difficult to even now obtain genuinely objective comment from the government on the potency of imprisonment. For totally different reasons the same is true of the public; they relate the issue of punishment too closely with the care of, or recompense for, the victims of crime and may themselves be guilty to a greater or lesser extent of 'revengism' and neither knowing nor caring what happens to those sentenced to a term of imprisonment. But perceptions are that if an offender is not sent to prison, that they 'got off'. [Michael Howard, 1995 consultation paper 'Strengthening Punishment in the Community']. Wrong though this may be, one can have some sympathy for that view, but a tough punishment does not necessarily mean a long prison sentence or a prison sentence at all. However, imprisonment has long been regarded as the most severe punishment the courts can impose, and it is wholly reasonable to suppose that those who are sentenced to a term at Her Majesty's

Pleasure should be seen to suffer some hardship and perhaps remain totally isolated from any means of pleasure; maybe to fill their time contemplating the error of their or undertaking hard physical labour thereby ensuring that the deviant will think twice about committing another crime with all the consequences which would flow therefrom, almost inevitably a further longer term inside. This should remain a deterrent but unfortunately this is not always the case.

Regrettably, and whatever the future of our prisons there will always be a requirement for secure places of detention as there are at large [and fortunately a number in detention] those who due to some mental incapacity are unable to bring their behaviour into line with what is regarded as socially acceptable; the psychopaths who will always pose a danger to others. At the date hereof, there are approximately 26,000 individuals detained in prisons who are regarded as having some recognised mental deficiency and who might, just might, be better off in hospital and who should not all be regarded as unreformed or unreformable characters but who for one reason or another do not receive the appropriate care. They may be redeemable, but either the regime has insufficient funds or lacks the will or the ability to provide the treatment the patient needs to provide these unfortunates with the care they need.

This essay will address the situation of those who are not beyond redemption and whether the answer could be decarceration and punishment within the community with suitable provision for rehabilitation.

What are the reasons for imposing a prison sentence on an offender and what is the offender [and society] supposed to gain thereby? Custody is imposed for several reasons; to punish, to prevent reoffending, to protect the public and to rehabilitate the offender. All to be done with humanity, respecting the prisoner's rights and his needs. All this is listed in the stated aims of the prison service. Let us examine each in turn.

To be sent to prison really means a term of enforced idleness. There is no compulsion to work but what work there is cannot be described as arduous; detention lifts from the detainee aby obligation to keep his family, to become involved in the daily routine of housekeeping, the search for or the maintenance of a job or otherwise providing for oneself. Food, clothing, heating, lighting and entertainment is all provided free but the down-side is that one is separated from one's family, generally of more concern to the older, more sensitive and intellectual of the inmates [the minority] and in them perhaps cause a build-up of resentment against the system. The environment is far from salubrious [as may be the company with a few notable exceptions] but is one in which certain mentalities may thrive. A stable personality will soon accommodate himself to his situation by diverting his attention [and energy] from his circumstances to some all-absorbing and lawful enterprise. NB; more enterprising minds manage to produce intoxicating beverages and provide other illegal stimulants on quite a substantial scale, and doubtless, if those involved were more inclined to use their skills legally outside the prison walls, they could do extremely well for themselves]. That apart, if our man can show neither subservience nor aggression towards his captors, he could probably manage his time constructively. [See Sykes, 1958 'The Society of Captives']. Incarceration may be for the few, but whether it is for the remainder is material for consideration and debate.

From the researcher's discussions with young offenders and their associates, it was established that they would rather do a short spell in prison that a long period of community service. Prior thereto, it was a fear of prison which had been of most concern. [See Cavadino and Dignan 1977 'The Penal System; an Introduction']. However, once inside it seemed 'a doddle; in other words, was no deterrent and quite contrary to Howard's assertion that 'prison works' and that community service was the soft option. [Cavadino ibid].

On the re-offending and protection of the public aspect, unless only totally reformed characters are released into the community then, with reconviction rates of over 50% [Home Office Statistical Bulletin June 1997] the crime statistics receive only a temporary reprieve until the non-reformed are released. *This is not exclusive to the UK* by any means; in fact, it is accepted *throughout the world* that prison does not reform. These figures cannot account for the number who would not have reoffended under any circumstances [the 'one-off' criminals] where the punishments whatever they were had no bearing on the post-release activities which were entirely within the law. Or apparently so.

So, what about the rehabilitative value of imprisonment? Within the prison system, there are several opportunities the inmate has to reform. He can address his offending behaviour, but it is doubtful many do. There are other worthwhile channels available for the prisoner to follow, e.g., substance-abuse counselling the value of which cannot be overstated bearing in mind that 80% of all offences are drug or alcohol related. Then there is education. Some establishments are well equipped for the latter option, and according to Jeffrey R Butcher, chairman, Association of Prison Education Contractors, '... the government needs to make its commitment to a rehabilitative prison system in which education has a vital role ...' With 60% of the prison population [63,550 in December 1997; in 2019, 87,600 or so] having literary and numerical skills at or below level one, they qualify for only 1 in 25 job vacancies; basic education therefore must be a top priority. In 1997/8 the prison education budget was £36.25m [Richard Tilt, Director General HM Prison Service]. But spending dropped by £2.5m over a period of twelve months [Butcher, ibid].

In May 2016, Dame Sally Coates, prisons' education minister, announced a plan to transform the standard of education in prisons across England and Wales and help prisoners get the skills and knowledge they need to turn away from crime. It follows the publication of a wide-ranging and independent review into prison education by Dame Sally, a former head teacher with over 30 years' experience of improving schools' performance. Evidence shows education and employment are critical in reducing reoffending and therefore cutting crime, yet just 1 in 4 prisoners enters employment on release from prison, compared with the current UK employment rate of 74.1 per cent. In addition, just 1 in 6 [16%] leave prison with an education or training placement. Dame Coates said;

> '... education should be at the heart of the prison system and I am reassured that so many people share my belief in the power of education to unlock potential and transform lives ...'

Somebody has worked this out for themselves - at last.

Now what of these places of detention? In 1995 the Archbishop of Canterbury, Dr George Carey in a speech to a prisons conference held in Lincoln, expressed deep concern about the scale on which we were resorting to imprisonment, referring to 'Howard's crowded jails' and he considered that only the most serious of crimes [regrettably he failed to define 'most serious crimes'] should qualify for a spell in jail. He conveniently pointed out that at the end of 1994 the number of people held [in prison] on remand stood at 12,400, of whom 60% were later acquitted or given non-custodial sentences and the projected figure for 2002 was 15,400. [Up-to-date figures for prison facts can be obtained from HM Probation and Prison Service website].

Two months before Carey's speech, Judge Stephen Tumim, then the Chief Inspector of Prisons, attacked the conditions in Leeds jail as 'an affront to human dignity'. He spoke of a general air of lethargy, drug abuse, poor security and a high rate of suicide with many of those characteristics to be found in other prisons. Staffing shortages he referred to are still to be found in jails today [2019] and were partly to blame. Indeed, there is currently running a Prison Governor Direct Entry scheme to help[reduce manning difficulties '... Managing ever-increasing complexity; leading by example ...'. It was never going to work. Prison officers are more in fear of being injured on duty that they are about losing their jobs, so no wonder there is a shortage and a high turn-over of staff.

In 1996, with Howard still convinced that prison works, he announced in a White Paper a £1bn prison building programme; in 1998 Prison service managers announced that they were braced for a population rise of up to 92,000, requiring 24 new prisons by 2005, each costing £80m to build, an £10m to run per annum. [Home Office report].The amount of money involved would make even the 'lock 'em up and chuck away the key' brigade blanch, and hard to defend in the face of more pressing financial needs, e.g., the NHS.

Few new prisons have been built recently [2019] and overcrowding is still a serious problem and now there is a more recent concern about the health-care provisions within our prisons. Brixton, for example, caused so much concern to Paul Boateng, prisons' minister, that he has twice visited the unit within two weeks; in the same month, October 1999, it was announced that up to 100 special 'neighbourhood prison hospitals' are to be constructed to house psychopaths [a good move; one can only hope that they get some treatment!]. Broadmoor high security hospital is going to merge with one of four local NHS hospitals, so concerned are they about the high number of suicides.

Returning to the short sentence debate, Owen Bowcott, Legal affairs correspondent of The Guardian, broke a story on 04 June 2019. 'Prison sentences of less than eight weeks should no longer be imposed by the courts, the Magistrates' Association is urging, in defiance of more radical government proposals. To redirect the debate on rehabilitation of offenders and prison overcrowding, the body that represents all magistrates in England and Wales has intervened to suggest that only very short sentences should be replaced. This spring, the justice secretary, David Gauke, made a clean break with traditional Conservative policy and suggested following Scotland's initiative [adopting a presumption against prison sentences of less than six months]. Short jail terms disrupt family lives and do little to reduce reoffending, Gauke said. Instead, tough community orders should be used, backed up by tagging. His proposed six-month sentence limit has not yet been out for consultation or incorporated into any parliamentary bill. The Magistrates' Association, which speaks on behalf of about 16,000 lay magistrates, argues that a distinction should be made between very short sentences of up to eight weeks and those of about six months. John Bache JP, national chair of the Association, said ...

> "If current provision of robust and effective community alternatives to custody could be guaranteed in all areas, this would increase sentencers' confidence. Once this is in place, the Association would support restrictions being placed on the use of immediate custody to support the Ministry of Justice in its aims to reduce the use of short prison sentences. Sentencers must retain a discretion to order immediate custody if existing orders have been breached and there are no appropriate alternatives, but otherwise sentences of up to eight weeks should be restricted so that they are only available in the most exceptional circumstances ..."

Magistrates could in future be required to give a community order, instead of a prison sentence of less than eight weeks, apart from when an offender has breached an existing order or where the offender is only in the UK for a few weeks so could not engage with community options. Magistrates can only impose prison sentences of up to six months for a single offence or up to a year for multiple offences. The justice secretary's proposals would effectively take away many of their sentencing powers. Magistrates can always send cases up to the crown court if they believe a longer prison sentence is required. The Association believes its eight-week limit ...

> "... could have a significant impact on reducing reoffending rates, as evidence suggests that very short prison sentences are very disruptive to the employment, accommodation and caring responsibilities of an offender, but offer limited opportunities for rehabilitation ...".

Offenders given a community sentence as an alternative to custody must receive adequate support and monitoring, the Association says, ensuring that breaches are dealt with promptly and

appropriately. It adds: *"We call on the Ministry of Justice to ensure sentencers can be confident in alternatives to custody being available, effective and robustly managed before any proposed change in law."*
A sharp decline in the use of community sentences has been a result of trust breaking down between Judges, Magistrates and the probation service after privatisation. [Report by the Centre for Justice Innovation].

So, there we have it; a prison system that is overcrowded, unable to provide the health care its inmates need, short-staffed, facing cuts in essential rehabilitative and educational services, high reconviction rates and set for a population rise which even Howard would have considered inconceivable. When he came up with his 'prison works' mantra back in 1993, there were only 42,000 inmates; the figure crept up to 95,000 and prisoners were then accommodated in police cells, as there were just no more places free in any prisons. Little wonder, therefore, that those inclined to the adverse influences within a prison are likely to have the offending instincts reinforced rather than diminished, being more amenable to the inmate-culture than the rehabilitative influences which should pertain within the walls, and, lacking the maturity others may display in rejecting, without one hopes, direct confrontation, the advances of others who would mould them into membership of any one of the subculture groups [Erikson, 1966] and thereby almost guaranteeing a rejection of any attempt at reform or rehabilitation but a certain recidivism as was the conclusion od Clemmer [The Prison Community' 1940]. Sorry, Howard, prison does not work except in one sense only, viz., people in prison lose all rights. If they cannot comply with society's rules they will not be entitled to its benefits. They should pay for their keep in prison by working; all sports and entertainment facilities should be removed from prison; all inmates to attend daily fitness classes, drug rehabilitation sessions and education classes. Non-UK nationals who break the law will be jailed and put to work until they have earned enough money to pay their repatriation costs. Owning a cat, being married, in a same-sex relationship or being a father will not stop repatriation. Habitually violent offenders will be jailed until they are too old to be a threat. All convicted criminals who remain clear of the criminal justice system for the periods set out in the Rehabilitation of Offenders' Act will have their records wiped clean so they can get a job.

It is hardly constructive to attack the prison system without considering worthwhile possible alternatives. These could range from fines to probation and community service. There now must be found some combination of these, suitably modified, and even more punitive variations to reflect the gravity of the more serious offences if the 'incarceration culture' so prevalent in the UK is to be abandoned. Or nearly so. This is not being soft on crime, pandering to the liberal consensus [Jack Straw, letter to the Telegraph, 28 July 1998]. People commit crimes for several reasons but whatever they are, commonsense dictates that reform is only possible if the formula which drove them to crime in the first place is altered and by far the most effective way to do this is through education. Most offenders who finish up in jail are in desperate need of a basic education and one can understand their frustration at being trapped by their own ignorance. It may be said that as society has already failed them, that society owes then something now and the benefits of turning the wrongdoer from crime will be reward enough.

However, it is perfectly possible that the wrongdoer is not himself aware that lack of education, ignorance of his circumstances, is to blame for his offending. Any Party manifesto should contain a promise that nobody shall leave school without a certain minimum level of education and social skills. The researcher's own 'draft manifesto' contains the following suggestion;

> ' ... No child will be allowed to leave school until he or she can read and write properly, do basic maths and hold a five-minute conversation with an adult and write an essay of 500 words on 'What I want to do when I leave school'. Syntax and punctuation will be marked; pass mark 70%. All classrooms will be fitted with CCTV coverage and the parents of children who misbehave will be called to the school to view the actions of their child / children and if no improvement is seen, then the parent will be obliged to attend school with their children.

Nigel Whiskin, Chief Executive of Crime Concern [the UK's main charity concerned with crime prevention] quoting from the 1997 British Crime Survey, said that crime is largely the handiwork of the young and in 1994 two-fifths of all offenders were aged under 21 years ... *with failure at school emerging as the outstanding characteristic of young offenders ...*' In a Radio 4 debate [2 November 1999] a listener argued that if he were paid £25.00 [probably more like £40 today, 2019] per week, a fraction of the cost of keeping a person in jail, he would be happy to employ the person and to train him in his own business. There might be thousands of like-minder employers, managers, owners, local and central government figures and departments who would benefit from such placements. In addition, there must be colleges all over the country with student training vacancies for almost every conceivable course. No less a person than Derek Lewis, the 1995 head of the prison service and a former director of Granada and Ford UK [and no friend of Michael Howard] was prepared to exploit his business contacts to help find employment for the thousands of inmates who leave prison each year or even to employ them whilst still in prison; it is a short step from allowing prisoners to live out or prison whilst taking up these employment opportunities. In fact, this is now [2019] being considered as a viable opportunity for inmates.

There are always jobs to be done on a non-paid basis for all manner of authorities and thee are presently artisans of every kind as well as professionals[doctors, lawyers, accountants, teachers] in prisons all over the country, themselves offenders, and who may now be grossly under-employed, their legal talents being largely wasted but could be put to good use on any kind of basis agreeable to society and the trades unions to help train inmates less fortunate them themselves. Further, there is no reason why the students could not take professional examinations whilst still serving.

Note; a Privy Council report of 27 May 2019 [reported in The Times] Layne - V - Attorney General before Lords Kerr, Wilson and Sumption and Lady Black and Lady Arden [2019 UKPC 11 judgement March 18th] a convicted murderer who obtained a number of legal qualifications whilst serving a prison sentence, appealed against the Bar Council's refusal to admit him to the Bar as a barrister. The appeal failed, but the decision by their Lordships was not unanimous. It might therefore be reasonable to assume that for any lesser conviction than murder, and the application might have succeeded. Lord Sumption, refusing the application, stated that, *without ruling out the possibility of an exceptional case justifying a different outcome, it was difficult to imagine that a criminal conviction for murder could ever be consistent with the status of a barrister.* Doubtless, therefore, with modestly different circumstances, and a slightly less ambitious aim, opportunities may be open to many with criminal convictions and who subsequently obtain academic achievements, or even for those who already hold professional qualifications when convicted, should not give up hope of ever being employed [or re-employed] in a new or their earlier professions.

With appropriate supervision, restrictions on movement, curfews and reporting obligations, there is no reason why a compulsory training programme could not work as more direct rehabilitation, and well away from the corrupting influences of hardened inmates all jammed together 24 hours per day and generally unsupervised.

But this is no mere fantasy; there is already more than a suggestion that this is the way ahead. Jack Straw in a further break with Howard's 'Prison Works' policies, and speaking to the Prison Reform Trust on 22 July 1998, said that prison governors should have greater flexibility to allow inmates temporary release in preparation for rehabilitation into the community and to find work or training in preparation for release. It is known that the British Army is now looking closely at the idea of trawling through some prisons in order to recruit suitable candidates. Nor is it beyond the wit on man to liaise with, for example, the Voluntary Service Overseas [VSO] to offer appropriate personnel with suitable skills an opportunity to work off their debt to society and able to show a proper CV at the expiration of their term of duty instead of forever having to explain to any prospective employer the long gap [or gaps] in their employment history.

There were some grandiose ideas of establishing some 'Boot Camps' to deliver the short, sharp shock, as was tried min the States but now abandoned there and here, and another scheme to make the offenders confront their victims. This was a Thames Valley initiative imported from New Zealand, a part of a restorative justice initiative and which has met with some success.

In an article 'Cut the Porridge, Save the Bread' [Cochrane, 1998] the possibility of reducing prison numbers in a co-ordinated, phased process touched on the concern the public might have for their own safety if offenders were left at [relative] liberty whilst undergoing some other punishment and rehabilitative process. Andrew Scull in his book 'Decarceration' went to great lengths to point out the dangers posed to the public of communities of deviants, delinquents and derelicts setting up within their midst. But this is an unreal concern for several reasons. Firstly, there would be a close monitoring of the clients by probation personnel, and secondly, according to Brody and Tarling ['Taking Offenders Out of Circulation' 1980, HORS No. 64] a 40% reduction in prison numbers would result in a 1.6% increase in criminal convictions; we assume convictions of the 40% or so then in the community . At first sight, this hardly constitutes a crime wave, but seems would certainly be an inconvenience to the crime victims. Further, and depending on the criteria under which the releases would be agreed, one would suppose, reasonably, that a convicted murderer or rapist with say, only about a year of a long sentence to go, might be a suitable candidate for this release scheme. Grist to the mill of the red-tops; *'Murderer / rapist released early from his ten year sentence'*. Clearly, some discretion and common-sense is needed; but would the early release make any difference to whether the person will reoffend? Food for thought. One assumes that every possible pre-release check would be made in such cases. It might also be worth considering whether the prison governor should have the power to release early a prisoner who may be very close to his earliest date of release [EDR].

Ultimately there will be the question of what to do with offenders who fail to knuckle down to a work / education regime in the community; to attend and behave during courses of instruction or otherwise comply with one -prison sentence conditions. Clearly other additional and more severe restrictions might be placed upon them until they realise that the best option is for them to comply. Whatever the more stringent conditions are applied, they must be punitive enough to ensure that conforming is the sensible course and sanctions could involve co-operation with parents or family; there could be curfews, more reporting to the police stations, banning from pubs, prohibition of purchasing alcohol, prevented from holding bank accounts or credit cards, removal of driving licenses, compulsory drug-testing, cancellation of passports and possibly a reduction in benefit payments. Each of these measures might for some reason have undesirable consequences where it will genuinely hinder the continuation of the offender's training and education, so there must be a degree of selectivity. Applying the sanctions should not be too difficult, bearing in mind that the civil authorities and law enforcement agencies can make life unpleasant for a bankrupt or a banned driver.

With the high number of offenders serving sentences of imprisonment [then 65,000] the Prison Reform Trust acknowledge that this leads to logistical and financial problems which Stephen Shaw [the then director of the PRT] argued leads to wider problems for society which is that if you cram more people into prison there is not the funding to set up regimes to help them lead a rewarding and socially acceptable way of life on release. Precisely. One wonders what Stephen would say about there now being nearly 88,000 prisoners! [2019].

Whatever the arguments one can find in favour of decarceration, [expounded in the next essay] and as with the decriminalisation of soft drugs or brothels, it is unlikely that the public could ever sanction such a move on any scale which they would find acceptable principally, possibly, due to their reluctance to have at large felons free to roam at will; we've been here before; victim in particular have more reason than most to be concerned and probably feeling that those who offended against them have 'got off'. [Howard, ibid]. They may have a point. Scull [ibid] seemed to regard it as unworkable, having at his fingertips all the available data gleaned from various experiments and projects relating thereto. So, regrettable though nit is, it appears that HM Government will continue to pay out very substantial amounts of cash with no discernible benefits except to warehouse convicts without their accruing the 'benefits' that imprisonment is supposed to provide. However, one thing is certain; society cannot afford to do this indefinitely; some options must be exercised and it is reassuring that schemes keep cropping up; all we need to do now is choose one or two and give them a try.

Progress, slow or otherwise, is perhaps to imprison only those guilty of the most serious crimes, to consider the remand prisoner and more use of parole and suspended sentences. Dr Carey again ...

> *'... Prison life can lessen people's sense of responsibility for their actions and reduce their self-respect both of which are fundamental to law-abiding citizens ...'*

Prison stigmatises and excludes offenders from being reintegrated into society. What better argument could there be for an in-depth study of the issues and an experimental decarceration period. Only when the general public can be persuaded to take a more objective view and the government a more practical approach to this question can real progress be made.

Bibliography

Butcher, J. Chairman, Association of Prison Education Contractors. Letter to the Telegraph, 17 December 1997.

Brody, S.R., and Tarling, R., 'Taking Offenders out of Circulation' Home Office research study, no. 64 [1980]

Carey, Dr G., Speech to Prisons' Conference, Lincoln [1995]

Cavadino, M. and Dignan, J. 'The Penal System, An Introduction [1997]

Clemmer, , D. 'The Prison Community' [1940]

Erikson, K.T., 'Wayward Puritans' [1966]

Home Office Statistical bulletin, June 1997

Howard, M., Speech to the Conservative Party Conference [1993]; Consultation paper – Strengthening Punishment in the Community [1995] White Paper [1996]

Lewis, D., Former head, HM Prison Service article Telegraph by David Millward, 10 April [1995]

Scull, A., 'Decarceration' [2nd Edition. [1983]

Shaw, J., Director, Prison Reform Trust; letter Telegraph, 11 March [1998]

Straw, J., Speech to Prison Reform Trust 22 July [1998] Letter to Telegraph, 28 July [1998]

Sykes, G., 'The Society of Captives' [1958]

Tilt, R., Director General, Prison Service letter to Telegraph, 22 December 1997]

Tumim, S., Report, Leeds Prison [1995]

Whiskin, N., Chief Executive, Crime Concern - quoting from British Crime Survey [1997]

Essay 2: Is there a case for significant Decarceration in England and Wales.

Abstract

This essay will look briefly at the development of prison as a form of punishment in England and Wales then explore its effectiveness.

The benefits and the disadvantaged thereof will be weighed as will the political aspects of penal policy. The pros and cons of significant Decarceration will be discussed and reference will be made to the situation in Germany and, where appropriate, comparisons will be drawn. This essay will conclude that decarceration is the only reasonable alternative in the face of overwhelming evidence and academic opinion that imprisonment does not achieve its objectives, is already prohibitively expensive and a rising prison population can only be accommodated with a comprehensive and cripplingly expensive prison building programme.

Incarceration as a form of punishment is a relatively modern concept. Although places of detention have existed since time immemorial in which to detain individuals for reasons which were principally social, economic or political, punishment took on other forms which had little to do with detention; it was inevitably directed against the physical being and no attempt was made to persuade the deviant to address his offending behaviour and little if any consideration was given to why people committed crimes, their education or rehabilitation. Most criminals were ...

> '... *punished with banishment, whipping, hanging or the pillory rather than confinement* [prisons were] *more of a place of confinement for debtors and those passing through the mills of justice that a place of punishment ...*'
> [Ingatieff, 1978 pp. 24, 28]

Even the most minor of crimes, by today's standards at least, attracted the harshest of penalties. But it was the public's growing abhorrence of the frequent and bloody spectacles [the Bloody Code] which led to the commuting of many sentences of death to that of transportation, generally for life, which came to account for as much as 70% of the Old bailey sentences. But it was not until the eighteenth century that the punitive system hitherto seen or regarded as so effective began to undergo a change due in principle to a breakdown of the penal codes, started with the earlier rethink on the death penalty, and the development of a range of modern control institutions began to emerge; the 'Great Incarceration'. It was Cohen in 'Visions of Social Control' [1984] who suggested the following changes in control of deviance and crime brought this about …

>[a] The decline of punishment involving the use of pain;
>
>[b] The increasing involvement of the state in deviancy control and the development of centralised bureaucratic apparatus for the control and punishment of crime and delinquency;
>
>[c] The increasing classification of deviant and dependent groups;
>
>[d] The increased segregation of deviants into asylums, penitentiaries, prisons, mental hospitals, reformatories and other closed institutions.

The result of all this was …

>'…prison emerges as the dominant instrument for changing undesirable behaviour and as the favoured form of punishment …' [Cohen, ibid, pp.13,14,25].

But there was concern, even at this early stage of development, that the conditions within these various institutions were primitive in the extreme where it was not uncommon for people to die of starvation and disease; where the warders were as corrupt as their charges, and with men, women and children herded together in the most unsanitary conditions. In the late eighteenth century and at a time when prisons were still becoming accepted as a punishment, a prison census by John Howard ['The State of the Prisons and an Account of the Principle Lazarettos in Europe' [first published in 1771] and in which he clearly set out his misgivings about the prison conditions in

England and Wales and which compared very unfavourably with those in some European countries, caused some concern and probably signalled the start of the prison reform movement. What is known is that the 'idea' behind these 'penitentiary houses' was ...

> '... sobriety, cleanliness, medical assistance, labour, solitary confinement, religious instruction [etc] to teach them the principles and practice of every Christian and moral duty ...'
> [Ignatieff [1978] p. 94 quoting Blackstone, [1823]

But it was clear there was a significant gulf, indeed a yawning chasm, between the idea and the actuality; in fact, and as will be discussed in more detail, it is realistic to suppose that the idea and the actuality never at any time in the history of the prison service even caught sight of one another.

What is apparent is that the move to incarceration as a form of punishment was not due to any social pressure based on evidence that the existing forms of punishment were ineffective, but that imprisonment was to bring greater benefit to deviants and thereby also to society; it was a convenient step and very probably the only step away from the existing menus of punishments. We know only that it was the *'dominant instrument'* [Cohen, ibid]. It is at this stage that we begin to see the emergence of accredited experts who ultimately developed monopolies in the care and control of deviants in their own fields of 'expertise'. [Cohen,1985 p 13].

But what brought about the change, apparently so desperately sought, if there was little to suggest the usual punishments were working? What was the rationale behind the process? There is a number of theories, the *orthodox*, mooted above, being that it was as a result of humanitarianism and reform, movement away from the barbarism so prevalent hitherto; then *voluntaristic* – to rationalise and regulate social life in accordance with emerging social and economic order; *deterministic* – changes in mode of production creating new class interests therefore changes in the forms and ideologies of punishment to support those interests principally the capitalist system; Foucault, an exponent of the 'new orthodoxy' theory which sought a routine, viz., labour, order and individualising of punishment, not less, but better to produce the 'disciplined subject'. The disciplinary regime acted not on the bodies of men nor their fears, but in the reform of their behaviour through subordination to the disciplined institution [Foucault, 1979. P.128].

Prisons were, therefore, a convenience for, et al, the accredited experts [see supra] and seem to have remained so ever since and, whereas they may have been close to accomplishing all the set out to do at some early stage in their history, that have a lamentably poor recent record of doing so. The stated aims of the prison service are to punish offenders by depriving them of their liberty, protect the public against re-offending, give the deviant the opportunity to address his offending behaviour and to undergo a degree of rehabilitation. [Home Office, 'Handbook, 'Information for Prisoners'].

However, reconviction rates of over 50%, average, with a disturbingly high figure of 75% for young, male offenders [HO Statistical Bulletin 5/97 [Reconviction of Prisoners discharged from prisons in 1993, England and Wales, 1977] is a clear-enough message that prison does not do sufficiently well what bit is supposed to do. The more comprehensive conclusions te be drawn from reconviction rates are that, whatever form imprisonment takes, it fails in its aim of rehabilitation; offenders 'grow out' of crime for reasons unconnected to punishment. Despite this, prison continues to be a punishment much favoured by the establishment.

> '... prison is a fiasco, and does not find defence in the celebrated purposes espoused in penal theory ...'
> [Mathiesen, 1990, p.19].

More specifically stated, the only rational explanation for the continued use of prison, arguably the least effective of all measures which are available to the sentencers is that more weight is given to ideological and political pressure that can be warranted, that it is a convenience, and it would be politically inept for any ruling party to do otherwise. Recent elections have shown that the crime issue can be a profitable horse to flog and the public, the electorate, seem to rally to the party rhetoric which declares that prison is where all criminals will finish up, and where they will stay for a long time; the reality is otherwise; that it only exacerbates the situation, ultimately doing no good at all for either society or the offenders. Further ...

> '...the basic evils of imprisonment are that it denies autonomy, degrades dignity, impairs or destroys self-reliance, inculcates authoritarian values, minimises the likelihood of beneficial interaction with one's peers, fractures family ties, destroys the family's economic stability and prejudices the prisoner's future prospects for improvement in economic and social status ...'
> [American Friends Service Committee, 1971 p. 33].

... which is succinctly put and applies just as much here in England and Wales as it does in the USA; *prison is counter-productive.*

Not surprisingly, the unease some observers have about incarceration has prompted them to raise many questions about its efficacy; the sociology of the prison attempts to answer these questions which in turn gives impetus to diverse movements which include:-

[a] Decriminalisation of society by restricting the reach of the criminal law;

[b] Diversion of the criminal away from the formal processing by the courts;

[c] The abandonment of the prison system and not least ...

[d] The decarceration of offenders away from prisons.

The latter aspect, as indeed with any of the others, does not by any means receive the universal acclaim as the answer to the problems which beset the prison service; two eminent writers on the subject were unstinting in their *criticism* ...

> ' ...this whole enterprise is built on a foundation of sand ... the claim that treatment in the community is more effective than institutionalisation is an empty one ...'
> [Scull, 1984 p. 1];
>
> And '... inevitably, decarceration seems to lead to new forms of intervention which reproduces in the community the very same coercive functions of the system they were designed to replace ...' [Cohen, 1979 p. 350].

And, what exactly is 'decarceration'? Scull defines it thus;

> 'A state sponsored policy of closing down asylums, prisons and reformatories and leaving deviants in the community ... because this is a more humane and effective means of rehabilitation'.

He goes on to say that decarceration follows demands for the pacification of the working class, increasing reliance on welfare as a major component for regulating the labour force and the emergence of a fiscal crisis of the state. [op cit., pp. 136, 137]. Very 1984 and Orwellian. This may be, but we are nearly twenty years down the road from these views which are flawed technically, linking too closely economic problems with the state responses, and empirically, as his experiences extended to mental hospital reductions, and not prisons.

Although this rather oversimplifies the issue, the basis point is quite clearly made but the next and logical question is 'why decarceration?'. Scull's definition refers only to rehabilitation, which we know from reconviction figures, is largely ineffective; we also have to consider best use of resources, cost, and a more academic question, 'why is England and Wales almost at the top of the European prison league? Morgan [1994, p.891] *'The countries with which we like to compare ourselves in Europe and elsewhere generally, make less use of imprisonment.'*

This is ammunition indeed for the exponents of penal reform who mare quick to point out that in Europe there is a developing a wide range of alternatives to custody. But behind this apparently simple device, Muncie and Sparks [1991, p. 92] point out that whatever comparisons can be made between different jurisdictions, they are likely to be fraught with complexities. There is therefore a need to treat simple comparisons with a degree of circumspection, but it does not detract totally from the argument that some lessons can be learned by studying alternative regimes and, more importantly, the available alternatives to imprisonment which are used in Europe and looking closely at their effectiveness. In Germany, for example, where there is a substantial reduction in prison numbers, [see infra] there is little to lead one to suppose that this has led to any noticeable increase in crime attributable to [as Scull might say] having deviants congregating in separate communities instead of prison cells.

The failure to rehabilitate may feature high on the list of matters which could be better addressed out of prison, there are other, equally weighty matters which will tend to support exponents of decarceration notably the rapidly-rising prison population and a need to build new prisons to accommodate them. The 1996 White Paper announced a £1bn build programme – denounced as inadequate by prison service managers, who were expecting a rise in numbers to 98,000 by 2015; and the cost [1996] of £24,000 pa. per inmate will, it is argued, be substantially more than the cost of rehabilitation in the community and delivered by already existing agencies.

To embark on a determined path to incarceration now will mean leaving behind a prison crisis where the rising numbers are forever pushing against the outer limits of the law and order budget, with overcrowding, worsening conditions, threats of rioting and disorder , where the Prison Education Contractors are having to operate with a reducing budget [1997/8, £36.35m, £2.5m less that previous years] these institutions will become little more that people-warehouses, with no budget for, and fewer opportunities to, undertake the core business for which the prisons were established.

Something has to change, and it is against this background that the idea of decarceration becomes an ever more realistic next step to the existing punishment regime, and the longer the crisis experienced today is allowed to continue with no realistic changes in the offing, the more disillusioned the prison staff will become and the more likely it is that there will be a repetition of the riots of the eighties [and later, as history shows]. To date, there has been only crisis management; without a radical new approach prison management will remain crisis management as is suggested by New Labour's audit of prisons.

The Federal Republic of Germany, with a place near the top of the prison numbers league only some twenty years ago, is a good example of the reductionism process and possibly because it was faced with a very expensive prison building programmes the UK is now. An almost imperceptible change in policy began to bring down numbers by 10% within five years. Initially it was a reduction in remand prisoners, then juveniles and finally sentenced prisoners. Feest [1991, p. 135] rejected economic reasons, demographic trends and legislative changes as well as changes in the crime rate [The police processed the same number of suspects]. Feest concluded;

> 'The reduction of the West German prison population is therefore clearly attributable to changes in the behaviour of the prosecutors and or Judges. It is what the Council of Europe call de facto as opposed to de jure decriminalisation ... it was a new mood developing amongst prosecutors and Judges; a recourse to handling of cases without format trial and dispensing with offenders in ways other than imprisonment.' [op. cit,p.135]

Whatever the urgency, there is little point in embarking upon a policy of decarceration unless there are in place some other agencies which will take on the task of rehabilitation, that is if we are to avoid the scenario described by Scull, who envisaged whole communities of social and mental inadequates, deviants, derelicts and delinquents, free to embark upon and continue virtually unchecked and terrorising members of the public going about their lawful business; where they might be 'no go' areas, so redolent of the ghettos of the US where drug-dealing and alcoholism would be rife on scales hitherto unimagined so driving up the crime rate taking them beyond the reach of all those who would undertake the rehabilitation process and subjecting them also to the violence and squalor that life in a ghetto inevitably attracts.

It certainly paints a black picture of America, but Brody and Tarling [Taking Offenders Out of Circulation, 1980, HO Report no. 64] consider that a reduction of 40% of prison numbers would result in a 1.6% increase in convictions. It is clearly not the intention to dump a whole bag of offenders onto the unsuspecting public without exercising some control over their movements, and here in the UK requisite agencies already exist albeit not perhaps on a scale equipped to deal with a substantially increased client base.

Decarceration means that we must employ a greater number of options to imprisonment. Bottoms [1983] draws attention to the *'neglected features of contemporary penal systems'* and acknowledges that there has been a proliferation of 'community' measures like probation, intermediate and community service and other developments like fines, suspended sentences and victim compensation. To that we have added a certain control measure , e.g., electronic tagging. [Criminal Justice Act 1991]. We have these agencies and options available already, and with the renaming and reshaping of the Probation Service [The Community Punishment and Rehabilitation Service] one might optimistically hope that it is being prepared for just such a scheme here. As with Germany, the beginnings may be with remand prisoner. In 1994 the number on remand stood at 12,400 of whom 60% were either acquitted or given non-custodial sentences. The projected figure for 2002 is 15,400 [Carey, Lincoln Prison conference, 1995].

And what harm would there be in looking at the number of prisoners serving sentences of less than six months? In 1998 the number was 37% of all prisoners, a staggering 23,500. For a regime which regards prison as a last resort for serious offenders, one wonders if a six-month sentence is appropriate punishment or whether, with a policy of decarceration as in West Germany, would unlock more options for the sentencers in these cases. If we continue to jail those who fall foul of the law and with no regard for the state of our prisons, then we can make one proud boast; that we will soon top the European prison league. The institutions will hop from one crisis to another and run the serious risk of both prisoner and staff unrest and force the government to embark on a massive recruiting and building programme. A billion here, a billion there ... soon we'll be talking big money.

But that's not all. We will be unable to afford the care the offender is entitled to; no education, no alcohol or drug abuse programmes, no addressing of his offending behaviour and no rehabilitation, no anger-management courses. We will, as has already been said, simple warehousing people. Treatment of offenders in this was is counter-productive. What will happen is the alienation of very large numbers of individuals who will return time and time again with the very real possibility that many of them will eventually attract life sentences. They must be given the opportunity with the help of outside agencies to grow out of criminal behaviour. With 60% of the prison population virtually illiterate and 80% of offences either alcohol or drug-related, a spell in jail is not what is needed but should it be necessary then nit must be combined with some rehabilitation programme, less and less affordable today as so much of the prisons budget is spent on prisoner accommodation and food, uniforms and prison staff.

It is high time that we took a leaf out of our neighbours' book; look sooner rather than later at a serious decarceration scheme.

Bibliography

American Friends Service Committee 'Struggle for Justice: A report on Crime and Punishment in America. New York, Hill and Wang [1971]

Brody, SR, and Tarling, R. 'The Effectiveness of Sentencing' Home Officer Research Study No. 35 London HMSO [1980]

Bottoms, AE, 'Neglected Features of Contemporary Penal Systems' in Garland , D and Young, P, [Eds] The Power to Punish; Contemporary Penalty and Social Analysis pp. 162 – 202 [1983]

Carey, G. Speech at Lincoln; Prison Officers Conference [1995]

Cohen, S. 'The Punitive City' Notes on the dispersal of social control' Contemporary Crises. Vol. 3 pp 339 -65 [1979].

Cohen, S. 'Visions of Social Control' Oxford; Polity Press [1984]

Feest, J. 'Reducing the Prison Population; lessons from the West German Experience' London; Tavistock [1991]

Foucault, M. 'Discipline and Punish; The Birth of the Prison' Harmondsworth, Penguin. [1979]

Howard, J. 'The State of Prisons[and an Account of the Principal Lazarettos in Europe' First published in 1771; Reprint of abridged 3rd edition 1929, London: J M Dent and Sons, Ltd. In Muncie, J, and Sparks, R. [Eds] 'Imprisonment: European Perspectives'. London, Harvester Wheatsheaf.

Ignatieff , M. 'A Just Measure of Pain: The Penitentiary in the Industrial Revolution' New York, Columbia University Press [1987].

Mathiesen, T. 'Prison on Trial' Sage, London. [1990]

Morgan, R, 'Imprisonment ' Maguire, M, and Morgan, R, and Reiner, R, the Oxford Handbook of Criminology, Clarendon Press, Oxford. [1994]

Muncie, J. and Sparks, R. [Eds] 'Imprisonment: European Perspectives' London: Harvester Wheatsheaf. [1991]

Scull, AT, 'Decarceration: Community treatment and the Deviant – A Radical View' New Jersey; Prentice Hall. [1984]

Essay 3: The Mentally Disordered Offender.

Mad or bad is the question posed by theorists when considering the conduct of psychopaths. If the question were answered, would any significant consequences ensue?

Abstract

This essay will attempt to answer the questions, 'what is mad, what is bad' and how the law defines madness and the state of mind and the behaviour of the psychopath. It will also explore why this is such a rich area for the law and psychiatry theorists in their endless pursuit of an answer to punishment and treatment problems. It will outline the options the courts have in dealing with psychopaths and whether the prison system or health services are individually or jointly able to deal with them. Finally,, on the basis of the texts herein it will address the question, 'does it make any difference whether the offender is mad or bad and is the outcome certain for either of the cases, or is it just a lottery played out by the lawyers and the doctors?

Mad; with disordered mind; insane; frenzied; extravagantly gay; [of person or conduct or idea] wholly foolish.

Madness is a matter of behavioural degree, but as the night of common-sense and conformity with the collective conscience darkens into antisocial behaviour and, ultimately, the blackness of insanity, the extreme of human mental disfunction, at what point on this scale does one cross the line into the area of madness? It is not a fixed point but a band within which those who have to decide the question can manoeuvre; and their decision will depend as much on their own characteristic oddities as it does on the circumstances and personality of the subject; definitions can only be at best loose guidelines, the dice thrown within the minds of those who have the responsibility of deciding.

The simplicity of the dictionary definition belies the complexity surrounding the process of categorising the person by his state of mind; the tangle of lego-medical interpretations are hardly helpful. Is the child savant or the brilliant mathematician mad? Can certifiable madness come and go? Can madness be brought on by an unfortunate mix of 'normal' circumstances? Is it the mean, cutting through the peaks and troughs of observed actions? Or can a single act in isolation be enough to attach this label to the perpetrator? Common sense and misunderstanding vie with each other to work towards the inevitable compromise. The answers are as crucial as the questions are difficult. But this is a confused area, a hotbed of controversy where psychiatric opinion does not match legal definition.

There are many people who are patently not normal, their abnormality manifesting itself in diverse ways, as harmless, as mere irrational opinion, the quietly mad or behaviour as shocking as anything an imaginative and uninhibited scriptwriter could devise. It is when they offend and engage their hitherto lawful lives with the cogs of the criminal justice process that concerns us, the mentally disordered offender [MDO] and those who are classified as psychopaths. Psychopathy is a relatively new classification which tends away from the previous assumption that low intelligence was inseparably linked to antisocial behaviour, that stupidity and badness go together. Psychopathy as a concept was first examined seriously some fifty years ago having been regarded as 'the mark of the criminal' [Sir David Henderson [1884–1965] with little consideration given to the possibility that it was an illness, the result of a weakness in the mental processes of the sufferer.

However, the Gowers Commission [1949-53] decided there was some legitimacy in the idea which the Butler Committee [Lord Butler] dismissed twenty years later as 'no longer a useful or meaningful concept'. Their solution was to apply the term 'personality disorder'. It seemed that the psychopath if in fact he ever existed, was to be shifted around from one class to another and as the law did not recognise as a legal entity a category recognised by the medical profession, they suffered punishment rather that treatment, a state of affairs which persisted until the term [and the state of] 'psychopathy' became recognised by the legislature, embodying a definition in the 1959 Mental Health Act, but adding that the patient ...'requires, or is susceptible to, treatment ...' to come within the definition, but amended by the 1983 Mental Health Act to exclude this provision.

For hundreds of years it has been accepted that 'madmen' should not be punished for their crimes but rather cared for in the community and the principle seems to have slipped into and out of fashion but in theory changed little over time. The Reed Report [1991] suggested that 'mentally disordered offenders should receive care and treatment from health and social services rather than in custodial care'. Laudable sentiments indeed but by no means universally accepted, as others suggest that the mentally disordered are bound to indulge in 'inappropriate, antisocial or dangerous actions. [Rubin, D, 1972]; is it implied that they should be restrained before they offend? Fortunately, the latter view does not prevail in our society and it is accepted that for MDOs, diversion and treatment, as opposed to punishment, remains the overriding criteria. [Peay, J.]

The irony kicks in with violent and sexual offences, where the treatment element may be reduced with a corresponding increase in the punitive factor, the justification being that it is necessary to 'protect the public from serious harm' and together with the provisions of the Crime [Sentences] Act 1997[s.2, mandatory life sentence for a second serious offence] begins to prise open some cracks in the accepted philosophy that therapeutic sentences are the better option for MDOs; a creeping penal control? The legal definition of mental disorder, courtesy of the 1883 MHA is disarmingly simple, but its interpretation has been a rich ground for debate between special interest groups;

> '... Mental illness, arrested or incomplete development of mind; psychopathic disorder and any other disorder or disability of mind ...'

> Psychopathic disorder is defined as 'a persistent disorder or disability of mind whether or not including significant impairment of intelligence resulting in abnormal aggressive or seriously irresponsible conduct on the part of the person concerned.'

Author's note; this definition would clearly include driving a motor vehicle at ridiculous speeds, in a dangerous manner, and e.g., with children and other passengers in the vehicle; should the offender be treated as mentally disordered and receive treatment? Or jailed?

It is this sub-category we are primarily concerned with, but the two definitions are categorically linked via the thread of 'mental illness' but regrettably and unhelpfully, 'mental illness' is not defined, being left to the medical and legal professions to argue and for a jury to decide with some help from the DHSS [A Consultative Document, Cmnd 7320]. In 1986 the DHSS again stepped in, this time with the Home Office [DHSS/HO 1986 para 12] to offer some clarification as to psychopathy with the view that ...

> ' ... psychopathic disorder is not a description of a single clinical disorder but a convenient label to describe a severe personality disorder which may show itself in a variety of attitudinal and interpersonal behavioural problems ...'

These legal definitions do not accord with the views of psychiatrists and with the Cope survey [1993] finding that the medical profession is split evenly on whether psychopathic disorder should even be in the MHA, i.e., even be regarded as a mental health problem, the student is soon immersed in controversy; when is a perpetrator of mad, aggressive or irresponsible behaviour of a serious degree not mad? And what about the 'madness' brought about by reason only of promiscuity or other immoral conduct, sexual deviancy or dependency on drugs? The MHA deals with this only by specifically excluding such behaviour coming within its provisions. Again, and understandably, the psychiatrists presumably those who do accept it as a disease of the mind, will say that such an exclusion thereby discounts treatment being offered to those unfortunates, the very people the psychiatrists regard as being the largest group who would benefit therefrom.

This is where we look for a supposition, a system of ideas to explain the behaviour of those who do come within its definition, but based on general principles, independent of the facts or the phenomena which have occurred. We try to theorise about why it happens and allow the due process to take its course. There are many theories, some genetically based such as the XYY syndrome, the 23rd chromosome pair, said to produce in males the unusual degree of aggression. In the USA several people had been acquitted of criminal charges on the basis that they were 'helpless victims of their inheritance' and should not be held responsible for their crimes [Atkinson, RL.]. Another is the Learning theory and Heredity, propounded by Hans Eysenck, which suggested some individuals [who may be labelled psychopaths] had limited ability to acquire sufficiently strong fear of guilt or reactions about antisocial impulses to restrain their expressions. Other theories suggest diet and Attention Deficit Hyperactivity Disorder [ADHD] may result in Antisocial Personality Disorder in adults; or for a significant number of those afflicted, psychopathy. [Feingold].

Mad or bad? For the purposes hereof there are two distinct classes of crime which could be committed by the offender. The first could be the most serious, that of murder, and secondly, something less than murder. The former on conviction will attract a sentence of life imprisonment, the only possible sentence a court can hand down for this offence should he be categorised as a person of sound mind. However, where there is some suggestion that the offender may be of unsound mind [our psychopath] then the first hurdle the defence team will have to overcome is proving it. The process will begin long before the offender goes anywhere near the court. Where there is a suspicion of illness, possibly detected by the police or the defendant's solicitor, a whole gamut of rules and procedures will kick-in, and inapplicable to the lucid offender, and for the protection principally for the MDO.

Under the Police and Criminal Evidence Act [PACE] 1984, the presence or suspicion of MD should trigger all the protections and additional rights to which the mentally vulnerable are entitled. A failure to identify [the MDO] may lead to wrongful conviction or [more appropriate] the failure to expose the MDO to the treatment he requires. [Peay, J.] The irony is that failure of the authorities to recognise the MDO and afford him all the rights to which he would be entitled may lead to an appeal against a subsequent conviction, thereby possibly achieving a better result from a defence point of view that would otherwise be possible.

The reality for the psychopath is that, by definition, he will have at least shown a propensity for persistent violent behaviour and unless he can be shown to be an unfortunate exhibitor of other symptoms of mental illness then he will, in view of the psychiatrists, be running just below or just above the surface of normality, whilst others will not recognise his psychopathic behaviour as meriting any special consideration; they might doubt the existence of any underlying medical condition, i.e., '... *little more than a moral judgement masquerading as clinical diagnosis ...*' [Prins 1991, citing Blackburn].

It is seemingly impossible to answer the question of whether an offender is a psychopath or whether he is just bad, but it is certain that to even come near to such a classification he will be an offender indulging in *aggressive behaviour or seriously irresponsible behaviour*, a legal category defined by persistently violent behaviour. This may suggest several things; firstly, he may well have been before a court on one of more occasions or he will be facing charges for a series of acts which fall within the definition and may include one or more charges of murder. In the absence of any indication that the offender is under any other disability so as to be either unfit to plea [The Criminal Procedure [Insanity] Act 1964] or able to pursue any of the other distractions open to those who display other categories of mental instability, the defence team will be deprived of the usual time-wasting [and lucrative for them] little diversions which may otherwise be possible.

It must be said that many [ultimately] classified as psychopaths are able to display quite contrary inclinations; Robert Mawdsley, the so-called 'real life Hannibal Lectar' and Ian Brady, the Moors Murderer, were both being regarded as possessing above-average intelligence. But intelligent client or otherwise, the defence will have to consider the consequences of following a route of having him categorised as a psychopath on a charge of murder as it may, from their point of view, be counter-productive. Conviction for that offence for a 'normal' defendant will attract a life sentence with a tariff date, i.e., an earliest date of release. On the other hand, for the psychopath, conviction could attract a Hospital Order under s. 37/41 MHA 1983, with the offender being sent to a special hospital with no time limit for release on the basis that he is suffering from a mental illness requiring special security on account of the danger he poses to the public. He could never be released. Nor does the court have to make a finding of guilt, as such orders can be made if the Magistrates or Judges in the Crown Court are satisfied that the alleged act with which the defendant is charged was committed by him. Convicted or otherwise, the order can still be made. This is termed a therapeutic as opposed to a punitive disposal, but for the accused it amounts to the same thing. Peter Sutcliffe [the Yorkshire Ripper] as with Mawdsley will probably never be released; the latter was a psychopath, the former probably also so classified.

For other offences, by far the majority, the psychopath exposes himself to another band of possible punishments apart from those which can be imposed on the 'normal' offender and which can be more punitive but which the courts are not obliged to follow; these are termed 'psychiatric disposals'.

In both cases, there remains the possibility of return to a secure, non-hospital environment should the 'patient' recover his mental health. Other options include a probation order with a condition of treatment whereby the accused attends a hospital as an out/in patient for treatment under a named or unnamed doctor. The patient may refuse treatment but must be certified as liable to benefit from the treatment should it be administered.

An added complication which can attach to the HO is the Restriction Order, under s.41 MHA 1984 which severely restricts the accused's right to discharge on the say-so of the RMO, such a decision now having to be made by the Home Secretary or a Mental Health Review Tribunal. The principle behind this limitation is that it injects into the disposal an element of public protection from the accused's possible future behaviour, as well as authorising necessary treatment which the court thinks the accused needs to treat any psychopathic tendencies; a 'double whammy', and this can be imposed indefinitely or for a fixed period which will depend on the nature of the offence and the offender. At this stage the courts leave the scene, with the fate of the patient being left to the doctors on the treatment side and the Home Secretary on the punitive side.

Whatever offence may have been committed, there will almost inevitably be some element of treatment included in his disposal, but, and as mooted above, [Peay], it is not always apparent exactly how the treatment is supposed to benefit the MDO. It may be the psychopathy, which is targeted, and which seems logical, but does it not also seem logical to address the behaviour, which is the manifestation of the elemental problem, i.e., the incapacity to control the predisposition to psychopathic outbursts? To answer this in the affirmative it removes any argument against not treating all other offenders, mentally disordered or not. The old 'treatability' element has previously returned [MHA 1959] relating to the definition of 'psychopathic disorder' [supra] but now in the Crime [Sentences] Act 1977, whereby a person of treatable psychopathic disorder could be sent directly to hospital [Hospital Direction Order].

This is not an easy subject to follow either from the point of view of the MDO, or those who must advise on the case, nor for the student of the subject. It depends on the interpretation of a plethora of contradictory opinion from professionals in the medical and legal fields who will, in the adversarial nature of the law, and the diverse complexity and depth of the various mental disorders which the patient/accused may display at time of trial of the alleged offence, have to wade through before coming to some agreement [unlikely] regarding the mental state of the accused or, more likely just agree to differ. It represents a maze whose various routes are indicated not by fixed boundaries or paths where countless other have trod, but by opinion constantly re-routing the traveller and by the circumstances and feelings of pity, revulsion or however their own mood takes them, or those responsible for the ultimate decision of whether the defendant is a psychopath. Then the accused will have to run the gauntlet of a jury, ever fickle, and who will decide upon his guilt or innocence. The court, and depending on these two decisions, first his state of mind then on guilt, may have open to it a second band of opportunity for disposal, treatment; [punishment being the first]. This raises another issue; is the psychopath regarded as being treatable? Here, once he steps out of the court he will embark upon a long, possibly lifelong, sentence in prison or hospital; he is on the edge of another maze. Depending on the turn he takes [or is led along] will depend on whether he will ever be a free man. He will be at the mercy of how others perceive him and his responses to countless stimuli.

It is far from an open and shut case; he could be freed soon, later or never. Consider Mawdsley; in Wakefield prison in 1977 he, with David Cheeseman [the latter in prison, remand homes or special hospitals since the age of nine for various acts of violence] killed another inmate, his second, David Francis, by garrotting him after torturing him and partly skinning him alive. Both were sentenced to life imprisonment. Cheeseman is likely to be released within the next two years [in say, 2003 or 2004]; Mawdsley will never be released; one of them at least took the right turn. If Shipman were classified as a psychopath [it is suggested that he murdered over two hundred of his patients] would he have ever been released? [in fact, he committed suicide in jail].

Psychopaths are categorised as such because of their persistent violent behaviour; what does a person have to do, how much violent or irresponsible behaviour does he have to indulge in before he is classed as a psychopath? Is all such behaviour necessarily psychopathic? When is it not so classified, were the offences those of somebody who is insane? Are psychopaths always psychopaths? Are they born or do they develop? Can they be cured? Whatever we have learned in this essay, we certainly have not answered those questions.
They are possibly unanswerable, but they raise plenty of opportunity for further imaginative discussion and endless hypothesising on the subject. For the psychiatrists and for the lawyers.

What we can conclude is, mad or bad, no significantly different consequences ensue for the offender; the white of the bad and the black of the mad who, to one extent or the other, collide with the criminal process, mixes in the eyes of those who have to deal with them into an almost impenetrable grey. The tragedy is that some are mad and bad, some just bad but others just mad. Some are none of these. But who is qualified to decide for them? To return to Mawdsley; Mr Justice Cantly, after sentencing Mawdsley for the Wakefield murders told him ...

> '... I make no recommendation about the minimum period of your detention because I see no point in doing so. At present I see no reason why you should ever be released, but it may be that something will happen which will enable you to be released at some time ...'
> [Guardian, 17 March 1979]

BIBLIOGRAPHY

Atkinson, RL. 'Introduction to Psychology' London; Harcourt, Brace and Janonvich. [1991]

Butler, Lord; 'Interim Report of the Committee on Mentally Abnormal

Offenders' Comnd; 5698 London, HMSO [1974]

Cope, R. 'A Survey of Forensic Psychiatrists Views on Psychopathic Disorder' Journal of Forensic Psychiatry. [1993]

DHSS and Home Office; 'Offenders suffering from Psychopathic Disorder' [Reed, J, Chairman] London, HMSO [1986]

Eysenck, H, 'The Scientific Study of Personality' London; Routledge and Keegan, P. [1957]

Feingold, BF, 'Why your Child is Hyperactive' NY Random House [1975]

Gowers Commission, [1949 to 1953]

Henderson, Sir David [1984 – 1965]

Peay, J. 'The Mentally Disordered Offender' Oxford handbook of Criminology, second edition, Maguire, Morgan and Rutter Eds.

Prins, H. 'Is Psychotic Disorder a Useful Clinical Concept? A perspective from England and Wales'. International Journal of Offender Therapy and Comparative Criminology'. [1991]

Reed Report 'Review of Health and Social Services for Mentally Disordered Offenders and Others Requiring Similar Services'. London; Dept. of Health, /Home Office.

Rubin, D, 'Predictions of Dangerousness in Mentally Ill Criminals', Archives of General Psychiatry [1972

Essay 3: To what extent should greater emphasis be placed on social crime prevention measures.

Abstract:

This essay will touch on the several methods employed in crime prevention and social crime prevention; it will look at the difficulties which may be encountered therein as well as assessing the effectiveness and value of each. Where appropriate, due regard will be given to how certain methods may be enhanced. The piece will conclude with an overall appraisal of the whole concept of social crime prevention, and whether it could just be soft-pedalling on crime and an easy option for the offender.

Of all the topics which come under the generic title of criminology, crime prevention is the one which excites a crescendo of indifference amongst the general public, except perhaps for the most anxious and consciously vulnerable, and the police who apply scant resources and fewer senior officers than the task warrants [Jones, et al, 'Democracy and Policing' [1984]]; it has, for the career cop, the glamour of a wet noodle. In the eyes of those not yet introduced to the inconvenience, expense or other, possibly more drastic and permanent consequences experienced by crime victims, it is a yawn; the cancer threat to the schoolboy smoker. To the householder it conjures up images of basic security precautions, boring routines grudgingly performed if at all, often ineffective and inadequate. Until they become victims. It is then that start to appreciate the problem society has created and they blame everyone but themselves knowing that they could have done more to protect their property. A candid summary might conclude that they, by their lack of appreciation of the problem, and their indifference to their own security, are as guilty as the perpetrators.

To an extent, society is to blame. It could be that our capitalist system stresses 'economic self-interest' as all important, rather than community spirit and public duty; everybody is out for what they can get, generally via legal means, but often illegally. In the glossy overlay we put on our lives, forging pattern, colour and texture of our choosing, crime is the bubble under the wallpaper. It can be shifted around but once there it stays. It is a fact of life. If we are not victims, our lives are peppered with irritations and expense directly attributable to crime.

It was in 1829 that the importance of crime prevention was made clear by Mayne [General Instructions for the Different Ranks of the Police Force] where he said ...

> 'The principle object to be attained is the prevention of crime. To this great end, every effort=t of the police is to be directed. The security of person and property, the preservation of the public tranquillity and all other objects of a Police Establishment will this be better effected that by the detention and punishment of the offender after he has succeeded in committing a crime ...'

[Quoted in IEA 'Zero Tolerance – Policing a Free Society']

Crime prevention is principally a series of defensive measures overflowing with initiatives not all structured o fit together to present an overall clear strategy to combat the problem; the gaps and weaknesses are exploited, successfully by the ingenuity of the more cerebral, or in ignorance by the opportunist and less successful criminals not awake to the defensive measures in place and which will ultimately lead to their being apprehended, so reinforcing the defender's belief that their strategy of situational measures are effective as a deterrence [Clarke et al 1988] and due regard to this must be given in the overall picture.

It may seem odd to any who have given it thought, that there are millions of people who turn eastward to pray, five times every day until body and soul part. Perhaps they regard this massive investment in time, and maybe sore knees, worth the expected return of a privileged place in the hereafter or reincarnation as a ferret or a giraffe. Yet in other societies, the upholders of the collective conscience cannot dissuade some minority classes from keeping their hands off the matches, the aerosol cans or other people's' property on a weekly or monthly basis or however frequently they may be inclined to indulge in criminogenic behaviour, the benefit of desisting being the right to participate in all aspect of community life and qualify for lifelong social security.

It is unlikely that the believers and the perpetrators of approximately three-quarters of all crimes in the UK, in essence juveniles and young adults, are behaving because of some quirk in their constitution but that the former have succumbed to social pressures and the latter have rejected any attempts by their parents or other authorities, their respective schools, the police or, for the seasoned performer, some corrective institution, to inculcate in them a respect for social convention sufficient to dissuade them from interfering with other people's property; perhaps on the other hand, no effort has been expended in that direction by anybody. Such efforts would be futile in the case of those psychologically or genetically predisposed to antisocial behaviour so we are limited to the consideration of those for whom social pressure and some form of punishment, or threat of it, will be effective. Why there should be success with our worshippers and none at all with our delinquents is difficult to ascertain, but from our point of view it is a useful exercise to contemplate; social pressure might or might not work, therefore how it is applied and the degree of success is what we need to explore.

But first it will be useful to consider the principle approaches to crime prevention which will be categorised as *defensive* and *offensive*. Defensive, or situational, measures per se ignore reform of the offender but undertake a series of approaches with the aim of protecting particular property with the unfortunate but natural consequence of 'shifting the bubble' [to somebody else's wallpaper]. Taken to extremes, it would see us becoming stockade dwellers, venturing out at our peril the only respite being the imprisonment of the perpetrators of crime, free otherwise to encourage others and failing to dissuade their offspring from following in their footsteps, in other words, to ensure in perpetuity the legacy of a criminal underclass, unaddressed for what cynics might call 'political expediency'. Pease, [1988] might suggest that the subject is cloaked in 'political rhetoric' and others might consider it to be a disastrous social policy towards offending behaviour; a climate in which we appear to reward the offender [whom some disciplines regard as the victim] rather than the law-abiding citizen.

Tackling crime in this way does prevent it to an extent and as the criminologists agree, has the effect of 'perpetrator displacement' on the basis that if the offender cannot offend against one person or his property then he might find a softer target or devise ever more ingenious and violent methods of enrichment. But whatever the defensive tactics employed, they have a totally negative effect on the potential victims and on the environment. The cost to the government and to the public via insurance premiums and protection of premises and the decaying quality of life, where whole estates are planned to 'design out' the hitherto easy access and escape for the criminals intent on their nefarious activities and to engender in the residents some pride in their surroundings sufficient to eliminate the 'broken window' syndrome [Wilson, et al, Atlantic Monthly. 29-38 [1982]]. It is unreasonable to suppose that we can deal with this by retreating behind walls. Situational measures may have one answer to part of the problem, but it is not the whole answer to all the problems. Ideally, we want to prick the bubble, or better still, prevent its eruption in the first place, not shove it onto somebody else's backyard.

With social crime prevention measures, we shift the emphasis from a victim to an offender-orientated strategy [Forrester, 1998] and from primary to secondary and tertiary measures being respectively to focus on groups at risk of becoming offenders especially those between the ages of ten and twenty-one [Home Office Digest 3 'Information on the Criminal Justice System in England and Wales – HO Research and Statistics Department [1995b]] and upon preventing offenders from reoffending, this latter task not being an easy one when dealing with those who do not 'grow out of crime' as , fortunately, most seem to do.

Society has limited options, but there are varying degrees of control as a principle theme, and include family, school, drugs, recreation [see main theme of this dissertation] and employment. One can add that getting into a meaningful relationship also helps; but perhaps that is a very temporary fix bearing in mind the very high number of divorces and domestic violence incidents. John Orr, former Chief Constable of the Strathclyde Police, when talking about his 'Spotlight Initiative' highlighted a number of points when he suggested that to concentrate on social problems such as underage drinking, transport, parks and public places, truancy, carrying of weapons, litter and public nuisance were all indications of, in summary, 'threshold crime' and control of these would men success in prevention. The figures proved him to be right.

In 'Crime and Deviance' [Rily, et al, 'Parental Supervision and Juvenile Delinquency] the authors suggest that parents should be proactive in relation to the possibility that their children will, or are very likely to be, involved in crime to one degree or other, and should take reasonable measures to keep their offspring usefully employed both physically and mentally; not by any means as easy as it sounds. But they are encouraged to discuss the consequences of law-breaking, and to be alert to unexpected or unexplained behaviour, nocturnal activity, lack of regular school reports. One might add [2019 update] unexplained wealth and gifts, bearing in mind the 'county lines' business; also there are frequently cases where parents, a single parent, especially a mother, is subjected to violent episodes from a child, and who are quite frankly frightened of him or her. On the site 'Reducing the Risk of Domestic Abuse' ...

> '... Child on Parent Violence [CPV] or Adolescent to Parent Violence and Abuse [APVA] is any behaviour used by a young person to control, dominate or coerce parents. It is intended to threaten and intimidate and puts family safety at risk. Whilst it is normal for adolescents to demonstrate healthy anger, conflict and frustration drawing their transition from childhood to adulthood, anger should not be confused with violence. Violence is about a range of behaviours including non-physical acts aimed at achieving ongoing control over another person by instilling fear ...'.

Responding to the signals of incipient adolescent delinquency, showing signs of disapproval of antisocial or criminal behaviour and themselves dropping double-standards is all said to help parents keep youngsters on the right side of the tracks. Parents are also encouraged to spend time with their teenagers, making home a place where they want to be, giving them space and privacy. This is an ideal. With many children whose parents are obliged by circumstances to work, or where there is just one parent, there is just not the time to indulge in these Utopian activities, where to concentrate on them would be to forego survivable income. An imbalance of priorities? Holdsworthy ['Crime amnd Deviance quoting Pearson, 'A history of Respectable Fears' [1992] pp 208-9] paints a black picture of parental care ...

> '... plumbing the depths of irresponsibility with shortage of authority in the home mirrored by the excessive leniency of the law ...' winding up to a fever-pitch of depressive pessimism with '... popular entertainment dragging down public morals; immovable pre-occupation with the erosion of social discipline; awesome spectre of crime and violence, perpetually spiralling upwards ...'

But there is reason to be concerned where young offenders find home a refuge from justice, an environment lacking in control, putting off the fateful day when they will have to face up to the consequences of their actions in the courts. With girls, Marsh [1987] suggests that there is more social control; girls are expected, by their parents in particular, to conform to a stricter morality, being allowed less freedom to go out onto the streets and to stay out late being a significant factor in reducing the likelihood of girls forming delinquent groups. Why should this not apply equally to boys? [Update; girls seem more likely today to form gangs and do as much as boys; however, girls are much more vulnerable to assault that boys, and with greater consequences; look at Louisa Peacock *'The dark side of female empowerment: The rise of Britain's 'gangster girls' running gangs]*

Orr [ibid], and perhaps tactfully, failed to mention parental control in his list, and indeed it would be a brave government which sought to legislate on how parents should bring up their children. It is generally accepted that a 'firm upbringing' by parents always pays dividends. It is not an easy path for the child or the parent, but what an opportunity the parents miss if they do not face up to their responsibilities, and what a legacy they leave for society in general and the law enforcement agencies in particular. The only realistic way parents can receive training is via a Parent Training Order, but only where a young person is already guilty of an offence. The second most influential authority in shaping the future of our children is the school. All too often the good influences of the home are severely tested at those schools where there is a discipline problem, or vice-versa, with parents becoming frustrated by the behavioural traits displayed by their children after a spell at school. Rutherford ['Growing out of Crime etc] in his study of twelve comprehensive school in inner London noticed ...

> '... marked differences in attainments and behaviour, systematically related to characteristics of the school as a social organisation which could be modified by staff, but also influenced by factors outside the control of teacher, i.e., the academic balance of the intakes. The schools' characteristics, i.e., set of values, attitudes, behaviour, disciplinary regime had a marked impact on pupils ...'

His conclusion was, that to a great extent the end-product of any school was shaped by the quality of that school. Again, this shows that there are opportunities to reduce the delinquent tendencies, to improve the educational standards of children and to ensure that those who need special attention do receive it. When we remind ourselves that 60% of all those in prison have reading and writing skills at or below skills agency level 1 [Tilt] does it not illustrate how effective or ineffective the educational establishments are? Or were in relation to those probably difficult pupils, and how society has failed them? The dysfunctional illiteracy rate is 23% which puts the UK as the second worst in Europe. This must be a societal failure.

Catching them young does help; Rutter, et al [Juvenile Delinquency; Theories and Perspectives] found that schools which expected children to care for their own resources had better behaved pupils, better attendance and less delinquency. Giving responsibility and trusting children at an early age seems to engender in them a maturity and common-sense, a foundation for later educational achievement. The authors found delinquency was a problem amongst the *least able*. [Update; consider the Black, Asian Minority Ethnic Groups [BAME] when looking at this issue]. A view is that these children should either be encouraged to do what they wanted to do, which mens a wider curriculum from which to select a more amenable series of subjects [perhaps more manual training such as woodworking, metalwork or even special physical education courses], or should be diverted via special needs staff to remove from them the feeling that they are already failures. Here is a chance to use the *word now* rather than the *sword later*.

An avenue followed successfully in France was the establishment of leisure facilities. [King, 1989]. Those who feel unable to cope with being 'shoehorned' by our education system into a middle-class mould which would hang uncomfortably round their shoulders, may be better occupied in more physical exertions once having mastered basic literacy [and numeracy] skills, to shine through sports opportunities offered by full-time, cheap and accessible recreational facilities, or practical training in artisan skills. Exercise brawn, not necessarily all brain, as in their case it may prove an easier route but without limiting horizons.

The above relate principally to the younger elements, to secondary measure, pre-offender individuals, though it would be naïve to assume that there are not a few offender-pupils who would benefit from the same kind of attention from both parents and teachers alike.

The drugs topic is interesting. The general perception is that three-quarters of all crime [probably more now, in 2019] is drug-related. [Mowlem, 2000]. If one were to include alcohol, the figure would be substantially higher, but to an extent, society is to blame because of the failure to properly address the inevitable, that soft drug use is so widespread and generally regarded as a 'social' habit, and no more harmful the smoking tobacco [!] but we continue to clog up our courts and prisons with inoffensive [?] cannabis [and probably ecstasy and LSD] users and small-time suppliers; if it is not so very wrong to smoke cannabis then why is it more wrong to supply it? [Utley, 2000]. This is a problem more so now bearing in mind the cost of keeping people in prison. [Update; it might be a useful exercise to establish whether the jailed users and suppliers also fall into the same educational-achievement category as most of the other prisoners or are [doubtful] better educated]. Maybe cannabis users should be treated in the same was as ASH treat or regard tobacco smokers, with firmer action, better resources and more cash allocated to the overall hard-drug problem. Narcotics are not that much different from alcohol and could, perhaps, be treated the same way. It is of some concern that the legislation covering the drug 'abuse' problem is nearly thirty years old [now updated to the Misuse of Drugs Act 1971 [Amendment] Order 2018 – look at the House of Lords debate, 21 November 2018]]. Decriminalisation might be the first step towards 'civilised' drug taking. It is a vice but can be accepted as mere human weakness if it affects only the drug taker. [Utley, ibid]. These sentiments are shared by many. And not shared by many.

This is perhaps a matter for the collective conscience, and the braver politicians to deal with, and in the meantime, while it is illegal to own or sell narcotics, it remains highly lucrative to the criminals who sell them, and burgling and mugging by the users, many of school age, and as certain sections of society will point out, by not 'legalising it' society will go on creating a criminal class by its intransigence in not confronting the issue in a 'sensible' way. [Update; for an indication of just how lucrative the drug business is, read the book *'Set Up!'* By Edd King [Amazon, kindle or paper-back; it is fiction, but a lot of the information on drug supply is fact-based].

Another important social crime-prevention measure is employment. The devil may find work for idle hands; an idle mind is the devil's workshop; it is generally accepted that in times of economic downturn, and therefore high unemployment, property offences increase. Dickinson [1994] noted a definite connection between burglary and unemployment, a finding borne out by ACOP. But there will always be employment problems on varying scales whatever the economy is doing. The young unemployed can certainly be diverted by training schemes to not only keep them busy but also to give them hope and will always be high on the agenda for any government; it is good for votes. But finding jobs is another matter. For those unfortunates who have a criminal record and especially those who have been in prison, there are special difficulties, principally because society seems to be unable to accept the theory of redemption; when a person has carried out his sentence that society has to accept him back, but is reluctant to do so. The idea has now been mooted that young offenders should be ;shadowed' by volunteers, backed by a £30,000 grant to the Youth Justice Board [YJB]. This is very possibly set to cause more problems than it will overcome, especially where the offender genuinely wants to go 'straight'. Many on being released from prison face life on the streets [Ramsbotham, 2000] and others were to be denied council accommodation [a policy now reversed].

These last issues are examples of social measures designed to exacerbate the problems, a smack in the face for the tertiary measures of social crime prevention. It needs little else to turn the offender back to crime, makes it very difficult to get jobs and generally makes them feel rejected by society - for life. Finding work for the young, for the released prisoner and the perpetrators of minor offences should be a priority.

But what do all these methods add up to? Firstly, it would be unrealistic to assume that social crime prevention methods alone are the answer to society's crime problem. They are not, as there will always be those who are totally immune to any kind of pressure to reform, and could thereby be diverted from offending, but what we do know is that pursuing initiatives on education and drug abuse alone will go a long way to cutting out more than half of all crime. We also know that social pressure is effective; criticism of behaviour by peers, and isolation by them or their associates who indulge in mindless acts of vandalism ['expressive property crime' the beginning] and more watchful parents and teachers will generally divert the potential criminal particularly on the 'early' offences.

Crime prevention costs money and to continue to treat the symptoms whilst failing to work on a synthesised strategy for social crime prevention means the cost of crime will soon be prohibitive. Already the various agencies manage on a crisis footing, and with ever-louder recycling of the political rhetoric militating against anything but prison as the answer, the quiet progress made by the exponents of social engineering will be trashed, flattened by the steamroller of political rabble-rousing which dare not count the cost of its policies. Social crime prevention measures mean giving common-sense a chance, which in turn means winning over the vociferous minority who are ever critical of anything but the conservative approaches towards the offender and the offending culture. Crime prevention must evolve; this means a new approach with new methods or variations on the old, but however hard we try, the reformists will not succeed in the long term without the support of society.

BIBLIOGRAPHY

ACOP 'Social Circumstances of Young Offenders under Supervision' Lancaster University [1993]

Clarke, RV. and Mayew, PM. 'Crime as Opportunity' HORS No.34 HMSO [1976]

CPV – Child on Parent Violence / APVA - Adolescent to Parent Violence and Abuse. Retrieved 07 June 2019 from https://www.reducingtherisk.org.uk/cms/content/child-parent-violence

DoE 'Code of Guidance for Local Authorities on the Allocation of Accommodation and Homelessness'

Dickinson, D. 'Crime and Unemployment' Cambridge Dept. of Applied Economics.

Forrester, D. and Chatterton, M. and Pease, K. 'The Kirkhold Burglary Prevention Project' CPUS Paper23 London, HO. [1990]

Home Office. 'Information on the Criminal Justice System in England and Wales'. Research and Statistics Dept. Digest 3. [1995]

Holdsworthy, S. 'Crime and Deviance' [quoting Pearson, G 'A History of Respectable Fears' pp. 208 – 9] [1992]

Jones, T, Newburn, T, Smith, DJ. 'Democracy and Policing' London: Policy Studies Institute. [1994]

King, M. 'Social Crime Prevention a la Thatcher' Howard Journal, Volume 28 No. 4 pp. 291-312 [1989]

Marsh, L. 'Sociology in Focus'; Crime' Longman, New Youk. [1987]

Mayne, Sir, R. 'General Instructions or the Different Ranks for the Police Force' Quoted in IEA 'Zero Tolerance Policing in a Free Society'

Mowlem, M. Home Affairs Minister, Radio 4 interview 16 May [2000]

Orr, J. Chief Constable, Strathclyde Police; Strathclyde; Spotlight Initiative'

Peacock. L. Gangster Girls. Retrieved from https://www.telegraph.co.uk/women/womens-life/10857716/Britains-gangster-girls-The-dark-side-of-female-empowerment-The-rise-of-women-and-females-running-gangs.html [June 2019

Pease, K. 'Crime Prevention' In Maguire, Morgan and Reiner, the Oxford Handbook of Criminology, OU press [1994]

Ramsbotham, D. Chief Inspector of Prisons, Report March 2000.

Rily, D and Shaw, M 'Parental Supervision and Juvenile Delinquincy' Home Office Research Study83; London HMNSO [1985]

Rutherford, A. 'Growing out of Crime – Society and Young People in Trouble' pp 117-8.

Rutter, M, and Giller, H. 'Juvenile Delinquency – Theories and Perspectives' Harmondsworth, Penguin.

Tilt, R. DG Prison Service. Letter Telegraph, 22 12 1997

Utley, T; Daily Telegraph. 29 March 2000.

Wilson, J and Kelling, G. 'Atlantic Monthly' pp 29 – 38 [1982

Printed in Poland
by Amazon Fulfillment
Poland Sp. z o.o., Wrocław